ENCOUNTER WITH JAPAN

ENCOUNTER
WITH
JAPAN

Herbert Passin

KODANSHA INTERNATIONAL LTD
Tokyo, New York and San Francisco

Distributed in the United States by Kodansha International/USA
Ltd., through Harper & Row, Publishers, Inc., 10 East 53rd Street,
New York, New York 10022.

Published by Kodansha International Ltd., 12–21, Otowa 2-chome,
Bunkyo-ku, Tokyo 112 and Kodansha International/USA Ltd., 10
East 53rd Street, New York, New York 10022 and 44 Montgomery
Street, San Francisco, California 94104.

LCC 82–48166
ISBN 0–87011–545–6
ISBN 4–7700–1050–8 (in Japan)

CONTENTS

All Japanese names referred to in the text are given in the Western order, with the family name last.

INTRODUCTION ✰

This is an account of one man's encounter with Japan. Every foreigner who comes to be involved with Japan has his own unique experience in this regard and, while these experiences share some common elements, I do not offer my own as prototypical in any sense. It is unique, following its own inner trajectory, its own interplay of cause and effect. It is only one of many possible encounters.

During World War II, both the American army and navy established schools for the study of Japanese. Thus, for the first time in history the United States placed Japanese squarely on the national agenda. It is one of those historical ironies that at the very same time Japan moved in the other direction, downplaying English as the language of the enemy.

It is also ironic that this unprecedented historical turn was the result of two highly undesirable developments. The first was the war itself. Japan was the enemy, and the fighting of a war requires a broad-spectrum ability to handle the enemy language on many different fronts.

The second was the effect of the war on the position of the Japanese-Americans. There were in the United States several hundreds of thousands of American citizens and residents of Japanese origin and, therefore, many tens of thousands, at least, who were able to handle the Japanese language. But this resource could not be fully used because the American people in general, and the authorities, military and civilian, in particular, did not trust them. The Japanese-Americans were considered, at least during the first period of the war, as a part of the enemy Japanese nation.

There was, of course, a strong element of racism in this, but racism was not all of it. German-Americans are not racially distinguishable from mainstream Americans, but during World War I, Americans of German descent also suffered discrimination and indignities. There was a period of great foolishness when it was considered patriotic to refuse to play music by German composers (including Beethoven) or to read books and poetry by German writers, when German-Americans Americanized their family names and sauerkraut was renamed "liberty cabbage." The German-Americans were never evacuated from their homes, as were the Japanese-Americans, but neither was it the case that their residences were so concentrated in geographical zones that were considered militarily sensitive. Remember that the Japanese-Americans were evacuated only from the West Coast; those living in other areas were neither evacuated nor obliged to move to relocation camps.

In any event, because of this situation, the armed forces trained several thousand Americans of non-Japanese descent. I was one of them. We were trained for a role in the prosecution of the war. How important we were in this regard is debatable. But it was the secondary outcomes of this training that turned out to be the most productive. The military language schools became the source of the great majority of the immediate postwar generation of Japan scholars in American universities and the trainers of the next generation. And during the earlier period, before U.S.–Japan relations developed on such a wide front, they were the main "communicators," to use a currently fashionable word.

8

Between the spring of 1944 and the end of the war, I was given a privilege in the guise of a military assignment, almost inconceivable to combat-age men in the warring countries: studying Japanese. During this period, millions of soldiers fought, were wounded, and died on battle fronts all over the world, and countless millions of civilians were killed or died passively without even the comfort of being able to pretend that they were defending themselves. My younger brother was a prisoner of war in Germany, having been shot down in the North Sea after a bombing raid on the Kiel Canal. But I and my fellow language students knew of these things only through a muffled haze as it were, through the media or through our own personal networks of friends, relatives, or fellows sharing the same attributes of race, religion, school, or national origin.

Altogether, we numbered several thousands, divided among the army and the navy. About six thousand in the army-trained group were Japanese-Americans, at first suspected of defective citizenship because of their racial ties to the enemy, and then only grudgingly accepted as full citizens and fellow soldiers. About two thousand of us were Americans of other descent. We were earmarked for officer status, the Japanese-Americans for enlisted status.

Although our assignment was seen as a cushy one by those sent to combat or consigned to the dull routines of noncombat military organization, it was not so intended by the designers of the program. We were being trained for what was perceived as a tough assignment: for combat intelligence with the troops; fighting the Imperial Japanese forces throughout Asia and the Pacific; handling prisoners; and the Occupation of Japan, which was seen as the certain outcome of the war. If our preparation was more agreeable, our destined military function was no less hazardous than any other combat function.

And indeed most of the early graduates ended up in combat-related positions throughout the Pacific. It was only the accident that the war ended before our training was over that kept me and my buddies out of combat. But that is the way it happened to end for my cohort: we spent our war learning Japanese and we ended up not having to fight.

This book describes that personal experience and its immediate aftermath, the first two years or so of my sojourn in Japan, that is, the period between spring 1944 and the end of 1947. It is not, therefore, an autobiography, although it has autobiographical elements. Nor is it a complete account even of those three-and-one-half years. I do not, for example, try to present a complete history of the Army Intensive Japanese Language School or of the first period of the Occupation of Japan. It is an account of my personal walk across the stage of these events, not an objective account; it describes the experience of my growing acquaintance with Japanese that developed in these various settings.

There are, I am sure, as many histories of the military language schools as there are language students who went through them. My language school is different from the language school that others experienced, and I have not tried to reconcile these different versions of reality. They are all valid, and they are all partial. Although we were equally exposed to certain common experiences, we came to them out of unique personal worlds that overlapped but were not identical. Our separate identities did not dissolve because of our common experiences. The language school was one thing to me because I came to it in my late twenties, a married man with a one-year-old child, an anthropologist with particular experiences, particular motives, and particular values. The twenty-year-olds not yet out of university, from a Southern background and interested in different things, lived in a different world even though we shared the same classrooms, teachers, textbooks, and dormitories. I do not think for a moment that my account in this book begins to describe their experience of the same events.

Nor was my experience of the Occupation the same as that of others. It was different not only from that of other Americans but also quite obviously from that of the Japanese people. The

fact that we Americans lived in comfort and in the euphoria of
victory and that most Japanese were having a hard time both in
their livelihood and in coming to terms with the defeat, made
for obvious differences. But early in my first assignment,
Fukuoka, it came home to me clearly that neither had all
Japanese experienced the postwar years in the same way. Some
suffered greatly, but others benefited. The beneficiaries were
not only the black marketeers or those who had hidden stocks
but also many simple farmers who were then in control of the
most important asset of all—food. And the farm families—hard
as it is to recall now that Japan is a highly urban and industrial
society—constituted almost one-half the population.

It is a pious commonplace to say that war changes
everybody's life. The usual implication is that the change is for
the worse. In the large sense, of course, this is true. One has only to think of the death and destruction—the countless personal
tragedies, the disruption of lives, the inhumanity, the genocide,
the maniacal arrogance—to realize that war is a tragedy for
mankind. But not necessarily for everybody. For some it is a
time of liberation, of opportunity: oppressed peoples for whom
war is a chance for independence; career military men for
whom it is an opportunity for rapid promotion or an occasion to
deploy unused skills; for businessmen to make money; for scientists to be funded at levels unimaginable in peacetime; for
engineers to create new technologies; for ordinary people to
rise above the petty boredom of their daily lives; for farmers to
alter the terms of trade in their favor; for small men to enjoy the
unwonted exercise of authority; for nations to experience a
sense of purpose.

I do not wish to leave the impression that I enjoyed the war.
Its tragedy remains a deep part of my being. But it certainly
changed my life. Instead of becoming an anthropologist
specializing in Latin America, I was turned in an entirely different direction. Ever since then my life has been deeply involved with Japan. Whether this change was for the better or
for the worse, what is certain is that my life has been different

from what it would otherwise have been and that I have become a different person.

Herbert Passin

Hama-moroiso,
Kanagawa Prefecture, 1982

I ✭

INTIMATIONS OF
JAPAN

Distant Echoes

Every foreigner has his own encounter with Japan. Each is a unique sequence of events that in benign retrospect appears almost fated. When looked at with a colder eye, the sequence turns out to be more like some Rube Goldberg contraption: at any given point along the way, if any one thing had not happened at that particular moment, then none of the rest could have followed. If I had not bumped into an old school buddy on the streets of Detroit, I would never have gone to the Army Intensive Japanese Language School. If I had not, while awaiting my draft call, taken a job with the War Relocation Authority and been stationed in Detroit, I would never have run into him. If I had not just had a son, my draft call would not have been delayed. There is an old Japanese phrase *en ga aru* ("to be connected"), which comes from the Buddhist concept of karmic connection. Perhaps this is what is meant by it.

Nevertheless, nothing less likely could have been imagined than that I should end up so closely involved with Japan. Until the age of twenty-five, I had practically no image of Japan in my mind, except the wispy half-dreams that come from *Madame*

13

Butterfly, a blur of colorful kimono, graceful bending of the body from the knee, and wigs of long black hair.

My only early childhood memory of Japan was of my parents (both of whom came to the United States from the Ukraine) occasionally speaking about the Russo-Japanese War of 1904–5. Many years later, when I had finally become a "specialist" on Japan, I came to learn of the impact the Russo-Japanese War had had on colonial peoples around the world. In the words of one historian of India, Percival Spear (in his *History of India*): "Japan's sensational defeat of Russia . . . caused Indian hearts to beat faster and youthful imaginations to kindle. As Lord Curzon [the Viceroy] himself remarked: 'The reverberations of that victory have gone like a thunderclap through the whispering galleries of the East.' " Louis Fischer wrote in the same vein about Indonesia (in *The Story of Indonesia*): "Never before had an Asian nation defeated a European country. Japan's victory over Russia gave a fillip to the national movements of the Orient. It meant: we can win; the whites are not invincible; let's bury our inferiority complexes."

But my first awareness was of its impact not in Asia but within Russia itself. To many of the liberals and revolutionaries of the period, Japan's defeat of Tsarist Russia was a welcome event, and it provided an important part of the background of the 1905 revolution. It may come as a surprise to many, particularly among the Japanese, but Lenin himself considered Japan on the side of the angels. "Progressive, advanced Asia has struck a blow at retarded reactionary Europe from which it cannot recover." As Louis Fischer has noted (*The Life of Lenin*): "He identified Japanese military prowess with progress. The Japanese military . . . had served the cause of liberty." "The capitulation of Port Arthur," Lenin said, "is the prologue to the capitulation of Tsardom." And Trotsky's summary judgment was that "the Russo-Japanese War hastened the outbreak of the 1905 revolution."

My mother was then a high school girl in Odessa, and she had felt, in the academy and among her friends, the deep thrill of hope that the Tsarist colossus was not invincible and that it might even one day be brought down.

But the peasant Jews of my father's village—he himself was the sixth generation of a family that had pioneered that village in the pale of settlement opened up by Queen Catherine the Great in the Ukraine at the end of the eighteenth century—did not share in Russian civilization. For them, the Russians—or more accurately the Ukrainians—were "them," as against "us." Every few years their neighbors in the Ukrainian villages would rise up in a mighty tide of superstitious bigotry and unleash a pogrom against the infidel, alien Jews in their midst. What my father remembered of the Russo-Japanese War was not the exciting political horizons opened by the Tsarist defeat, which had so stirred my mother and her urban intellectual friends, but rather the simpler delight that "they" had been defeated and gratitude to those Japanese, whoever they might be, who beat them.

The war, however, had two important repercussions in my father's little world. First, many young men were called up for conscription into the army. Although the infamous *rekruchina* system, which impressed eight- to ten-year-old boys into the military, had been abolished in 1856, teen-agers were still being force-drafted without regard for the situation of their families. In order to escape military service, desperate expedients were resorted to—buying your way out of the service, equipping yourself with false papers, escaping to another part of the country, or emigrating to America, the dreamland over the seas where the streets were paved with gold and the Jews were treated like human beings. Because of the Russo-Japanese War, therefore, the United States first came into my father's vision of a possible future life.

The second repercussion was a pogrom. The Ukrainian peasants, furious at the defeat of their country and the humiliation of their "little Father," the Tsar, were in the market for scapegoats and, as usual in Eastern Europe, the Jews were heaven-sent for that purpose. It was common practice for the

Russian Tsarist government to deflect the anger of the masses by directing them into pogroms against the Jews, often led by their local priests. Major pogroms encouraged by government took place in 1881–82, 1903, and 1905. The Ukrainians were Catholics rather than Russian Orthodox, and the neighbors of my father's village, egged on by their Catholic priests, poured into the village on both horse and foot, burning houses, setting horses and cattle loose, and beating every single person—man, woman, and child—they could lay their hands on.

My father's generation, however, was not as easily intimidated as an earlier generation might have been. The ex-soldiers back from the war and the sturdy young men of the village organized themselves in strong defensive formations, and well before the first night was over they had driven the Ukrainian peasants back to their villages, never again to return. The next time my father's village was ever attacked was almost forty years later, but this time it was by the German Nazis when they occupied the Ukraine. There were no survivors.

When dawn broke the next day, parts of the village lay in ruins, there were fires everywhere, but no one had been killed in spite of the beatings, and the villagers had ended the night of holocaust with mixed feelings of triumph and bitterness. It was wonderful to win, but what could one say about a world where it was necessary to win that way? The experience made it plain to many, including my father and his family, that they could not remain there much longer. From then on, all efforts were bent toward going to America.

In a sense, then, my life had already been profoundly affected by Japan without my being aware of it, in fact, even before I was born. Because Japan defeated Russia, Ukrainian peasants unleashed a pogrom against my father's village and, in consequence, my father eventually went to America, and in the course of time I was born there.

Some Glancing Contacts

Despite this prenatal predestination, as it were, the number of times Japan had even so much as crossed my mind could be counted on the fingers of one hand. Because I had been a balletomane in high school, I knew, for example, that the dancer Sono Ōsato was Japanese, and I often thought to myself that she was quite the most beautiful creature I had ever seen. During my high school days in Chicago, it had been the policy of the main concert halls to allow music students to see the performances free in return for ushering. For the more popular performances long lines of anxious students would form at the employees' entrance at Orchestra Hall, or the Auditorium, for the privilege of being selected to usher.

The dignified, white-haired chief usher—in the daytime a salesman somewhere, I believe—would take as many young people as he needed to do the ushering, and the others would be turned away disappointed, to try again, perhaps arriving earlier for the queue, another night. On especially grand occasions, such as the world premiere of Gertrude Stein's opera *Four Saints in Three Acts*, when Gertrude Stein herself, her inseparable companion Alice B. Toklas, and the opera's composer Virgil Thomson were all there, or the performances of the Ballet Russe de Monte Carlo, the lines of aspirants stretched all the way around the block, and our soft-hearted chief usher would practically open the floodgates. "You!" he would say, stern-faced and gruff-voiced, "See those door hinges over there? Your job is to watch them carefully. If they fall off, you call me immediately; and be quick about it! Understand?" In this way, he managed to let in three times as many eager students as the ushering actually required.

In my own case, I was lucky. The chief usher had—or so it seemed to us on the outside—his own inner clique who held first claim on the choice spots, and my younger brother was a member. Occasionally, therefore, he would see to it that I was selected, in spite of the competition. On the opening night of *Four Saints in Three Acts*, I was assigned as usher for the box that Gertrude Stein and her party used, and the memory of that momentary closeness to divinity, the smiling face a startling tomato-red, the gown a stiff brownish-red velvet, still remains with me.

But the two weeks the Ballet Russe came to Chicago every year were the high point, and I was usually lucky enough to be able to go to every performance, both matinee and evening. The regular ushers, especially the ballet enthusiasts among us, came to know many of the dancers, particularly the young girls and their families. I frequently saw Sono Osato with her mother and her younger sister, then fourteen years old, I believe, and, if anything, even more ravishing than Sono.

This glancing contact did not, however, arouse my interest in Japan, but simply fit into what I was learning about ballet, namely that "Russian ballet" was a genre rather than a kind of folk dance only for Russians. The presence of an Osato among the Riabouchinskayas, Danilovas, and Tounamovas in the Ballet Russe de Monte Carlo struck me as exotic, but no more so than the presence of the Norwegian Vera Zorina.

It was at the University of Chicago that I came face to face with Japanese for the first time, both of them fellow students. The first, the daughter of a Japanese diplomat father and a Scandinavian mother, intimidated me by her beauty. Tantalizing hints of worlds beyond my imagining actually lived in, of completely different thoughts, movements, colors, sounds, signs, and smells arose from the very fact of her mixed ancestry. She carried about her a mysterious aroma of old Tokyo, Kyoto, Hongkong; but, strangely, of an old-world sophisticated Scandinavia as well. Eventually she married a fellow student and both became professional anthropologists at one of the better state universities. The other was easier to know: a California-born Nisei (second-generation Japanese-American), she spoke in more familiar accents, and she was married to a fellow student. (He later became a special advisor on language reform to the American Occupation when I was also there.)

There was, within the atmosphere of the University of Chicago's anthropology department, some awareness of Japan, and students could not be wholly unresponsive to it. Frederick

18

Starr, one of the earliest anthropologists at the university, had already started visiting Japan early in the twentieth century. Starr—or "Dr. Amulet" (*Fuda-Hakase*), as he came to be known in Japan—had made innumerable field trips to Japan and had written many books and articles. A compilation of ethnographic travel articles that he wrote in serial form for the Osaka *Asahi Shimbun* newspaper in 1917, "Wanderings through Sanyō" (*Sanyō angya*), was at one time widely known in Japan. His English-language articles on Japan were confined, for the main part, to obscure scholarly journals in the United States.

But Starr had little effect on my own development for two reasons. First, by the time I was a student at the University of Chicago, he had already long been off the scene, so I never met him or took any classes with him. Second, he was in our eyes an old-fashioned type, a "mere" ethnographer who knew nothing about theory. We were at the time caught up in the exciting early controversies that have since shaped modern anthropology—functionalism *versus* diffusion, configuration *versus* shreds-and-patches theory, Freudianism *versus* behaviorism, structuralism *versus* exoticism. Our heroes were A. R. Radcliffe-Brown, Robert Redfield, Bronislaw Malinowski, Ruth Benedict, and Edward Sapir. The leisurely old-fashioned type of anthropology represented by Starr held no interest for us.

Some time in 1946, soon after I first came to Japan, I happened to be wandering with a friend in the vicinity of Waka-kusayama ("Young Grass Mountain"), outside of Japan's eighth-century capital of Nara, and we ran into what announced itself as a "sex museum." It was a fine example of traditional farm-house style, perhaps the house of a *shōya*, or local headman of the Tokugawa period, converted into a museum and housing a random collection of artifacts, pictures, and documents in dusty glass cases. But in the front garden there was a statue of Fuda-Hakase, Dr. Amulet. When I suddenly realized that Fuda-Hakase was our very own Professor Starr and that he had been sufficiently well liked in Japan to rate a museum in his name —even if only a sex museum—I felt a surge of pride in the

19

University of Chicago, and then shame that I had not paid more attention to him during my student days.

Much closer to the awareness of my generation of anthropology students was the work of John Embree, who took his Ph.D. at the University of Chicago. His study of the village of Suye-mura in the southern prefecture of Kumamoto was the first, and for a long time, the only socioanthropological study of Japan by a foreigner using modern methods of observation and a modern theoretical framework.

But what stayed with me from Embree's book was not so much the Japan that he described as the confirmation that the Redfield concept of the "peasant society," that is, the ideal type that lay in the middle of his continuum of "folk society" to "urban civilization," was a viable scientific entity that fit not only the specific places where Redfield had developed it during his field work—Tepoztlán (Mexico), Yucatán, and Guatemala—but any time and any place in the world. Some of our seniors did similar studies in French Canada or Guatemala, so Embree's study of a Japanese village was only another in the unfolding series of studies that seemed to confirm the validity of the Redfieldian paradigm to which I, like many of the others in the then new field of social anthropology, was committed. The term "social anthropology," which in fact originally came from the British anthropologists, was our proudly proclaimed label to distinguish ourselves from the hitherto dominant tendencies in American anthropology: the shreds-and-patches ethnographers, the diffusionists, the cultural-historians, and the social evolutionists on the one hand, and the "cultural anthropologists" on the other. The fact that A. R. Radcliffe-Brown, the distinguished British social anthropologist, himself virtually the founder of social anthropology, was in residence as a visiting professor during my first year at the University of Chicago, 1936–37, was of decisive importance in this development.

Embree's study, therefore, taught me much about theory, but little about Japan itself. When I first came to Japan, however, I realize that I had in fact been unwittingly influenced

20

by him. My first analytic paper on Japan, which I titled something like "Japan: Between Folk and Urban," argued that it was impossible to understand Japan unless one understood the important role that folk and peasant elements continued to play even in urban life. I would not today defend that argument as I conceived it in 1946; I wish here only to record the historical fact that the Redfieldian theory, and its elaboration by Embree, strongly influenced my initial perceptions of Japan, and the emphasis on the folk aspects led me to an interest in Kunio Yanagita, the *doyen* of the field that is usually translated as "folklore" (*minzoku gaku*) in Japan, but is perhaps better rendered as "folk anthropology."

In 1947—if I may run slightly ahead of my story—when I was chief of the Public Opinion and Sociological Research Division of the Occupation, Suye-mura was included as one of the sample villages we studied in connection with the land reform program. As matters worked out, Suye was not one of the villages that I myself visited. In the allocation of sample points among the several survey teams into which we had divided ourselves, my areas fell elsewhere. In fact, I have never been to Suye, although it was, from an early point, such an important intellectual marker on the path of my involvement with Japan.

The first time I tasted Japanese food was at the age of twenty-one, when Saul Bellow and I had our double-wedding dinner in a Japanese restaurant. Bellow had been one of my close friends since high school days. Our girlfriends had been roommates at the University of Chicago—his in social work, mine in psychology. We all decided to get married and to do it at the same time.

It was the year end of 1937, and Illinois State law required a medical test, which took several days to process. But the neighboring state of Indiana had no such rule, so on the last day of the year, without seeking permission or even notifying our parents, we piled into my bride-to-be's 1934 Ford and drove to a justice of the peace in Michigan City, Indiana, about two hours from Chicago. After the ceremony we drove back to Chicago and decided that since the occasion was so special we should do something special to celebrate it. "Let's go Japanese," Saul suggested. There was at that time only one Japanese restaurant in Chicago, the Wisteria Inn, on the Near North Side, and Saul had been there before. I had not.

"Japanese food?" I asked warily. "Isn't that raw fish and stuff like that?"

"You're supposed to be an anthropologist," Saul chided me, "ready for any adventure, and here you are balking at a little Japanese food." So we went to the Wisteria Inn and, as I recall, the plumpish matronly madam clucked over us newlyweds like a mother hen, encouraging us to drink a lot of saké and eat a lot of tasty little dishes. The main impression this experience left me with was that shrimp *tempura* was a very tasty dish. Considering that fish, and particularly raw fish, *sashimi*, is today virtually my favorite food, I recall these events with the odd feeling that they must have happened to somebody else. The first time I tasted *sashimi*, which was in Fukuoka City's Western Park (Nishi Kōen) in 1946, all I could think was, "Where has this been all of my life!"

These few experiences, if such they can be called, are hardly worth the recounting, except to demonstrate a negative point, namely that slight as was general American contact with Japan before the war, my own personal contact was even slighter. My first foreign area as a fledgling anthropologist was Latin America. I had lived with the Tarahumara Indian tribe in Mexico for a year. I had learned Spanish fluently and Tarahumara somewhat less so, and every indication was that I would continue down that path for a good part of my life. In September 1941, I started on my first teaching position, in the anthropology department at Northwestern University.

The War

Although the European war had already been on for some time, it was only when I had been in Mexico that it first really came home to me. As with many other Americans, the months of the

22

"phony war" had left me both very cynical and unconvinced that the war was serious. During my radical student days I had taken the Oxford Oath—not to fight for king or country—and while I found the Nazi moves in Europe disturbing, the phony war did little to shake my primitive pacifism.

It was the fall of France that did it. I was in Chihuahua City drinking beer and tequila with Mexican schoolteacher friends, several of them very active communists, when the news came, and I remember that we all, even the communists, felt a chill come over us, as if the cold finger of history had just touched us. The next moment I found it hard to remember the cynical pacifist arguments that had seemed so convincing to me the instant before. The communists still argued, although with markedly diminished conviction, that the war was an imperialist one, and they held to this official line until the Nazi invasion of the Soviet Union in September, when in a twinkling its "essential nature" changed. From then on, we saw eye to eye.

But Japan had still not entered my picture of the world. The war to me was Europe, the enemy Hitler. In December 1941, four months after I had started my first teaching job at Northwestern University, the news of Pearl Harbor came to me as a surprise—lying in my warm bath that Sunday morning reading the newspapers—because I had been so busy following the European war that I knew practically nothing about the Pacific.

My first reaction was almost one of gratitude to the Japanese for having given us the excuse we needed to get into the European war, where, like many other Americans at the time, I thought we should be. And had the argument crossed my mind that Roosevelt had tricked the Japanese into striking the first blow, I would have had no objection whatsoever. By then, the first hard news about the Nazi extermination of the Jews of Europe was beginning to reach an unbelieving world, and it suddenly became appalling that America should do nothing about it. The general public was still largely isolationist, the

America First movement was strong, the concept of "fortress America" was deeply entrenched, and "Lend-Lease" was President Roosevelt's brilliant device—or even trick, I did not mind—to supply the Allies in spite of the reluctance and heel dragging of the Congress. The Nazis had been meticulous about avoiding incidents that would provoke the American public too far, but Japan had done it.

It was with mixed emotions, therefore, that I met my classes the following day and dismissed them. "I am sure we all have many more important things than anthropology to think about today." The students were grateful.

Pearl Harbor brought not only the shock of war but also a decisive change to my life. How decisive, I was not to know until much later. At the end of my first year of teaching, I came into contact with the field of survey research for the first time. At the invitation of Angus Campbell, a social-psychologist colleague at Northwestern, I joined the Program Surveys Division (PSD) located in the Bureau of Agricultural Economics of the United States Department of Agriculture. The PSD, after the war, moved lock, stock, and barrel over to the University of Michigan, where it became the Institute of Survey Research, perhaps America's leading survey organization, and eventually Campbell became its director.

The experience was responsible for my later appointment in the Occupation to public opinion and sociological research and gave me a permanent interest in rural sociology, which I was able to indulge in studies associated with the land reform program in Japan.

In 1943 I quit my job in the expectation that I would soon be drafted into the army. I wanted to do a little more work on my Tarahumara materials while they were still fresh in my mind and to spend some time with my wife and newborn son. Once in the army, I figured, there was not likely to be much time for either scholarly work or for family. I totted up my savings and calculated that I had about three months' worth. Before the three months were up, the Selective Service System issued a regulation deferring fathers with dependent children for the time being. I was delighted to be able to delay the termination of my civilian life.

But three months turned into four, and four into five, and soon I was running out of money. I thereupon decided that I had better get a job to support the family until I actually went into the service. For a deferred able-bodied man, however, getting a job was no easy matter. Universities, companies, and government agencies—the most likely places for an anthropologist to find a job—were reluctant to hire someone who might be called into military service at any time.

Other than the financial question, my personal circumstances were extremely agreeable. I lived with my wife and baby boy on the second floor of a crumbling old mansion in the elegant Chicago North Shore suburb of Evanston. The mansion was owned by a retired judge, who lived in one wing and looked at least as old as the mansion and was slowly turning to dust, surrounded by his memories and old furniture. He was looked after by his faithful daughter-in-law, who was estranged from his son, and as long as she was there, the son absolutely refused to visit his father.

The house occupied an entire city block and sat amid decaying gardens that had once upon a time been lovingly tended by skilled gardeners. There was a formal English garden, a "tropical garden," and a Japanese garden, and almost all of the trees and flowering plants had been brought from abroad. During the cherry blossom season, which in cold Chicago was May, the Japanese garden burst into a stormy pink, and in autumn the flaming Japanese maples took on their winter hue. The main room had a fireplace—which was the only source of heat—and to sit there writing and look out from time to time on the lovely garden colors while other men of my generation were going into the armed services was an ineffable privilege, a moment of deep quiet in the midst of a world caught up in war.

The Japanese-Americans

But it could not last because my money was almost gone. It was at this point that I ran into a childhood friend who suggested that I try the War Relocation Authority, which was handling the Japanese-Americans expelled from the West Coast states. They were first, it will be remembered, moved out lock, stock, and barrel from California, Oregon, and Washington into ten concentration camps in the western and southwestern states, and then later, very gradually, those who received the proper clearances were allowed to move to other parts of the country. Several anthropologists worked for the authority, mainly in the camps: the theory seems to have been that the Japanese were so strange that you needed anthropologists—specialists in exotic, non-Western peoples—to handle them.

To my surprise my application for a job was accepted. But instead of being sent out to a camp, as I had expected, I was sent to Detroit. My job was to find work for the Japanese-Americans, locate housing for them, and, in general, act as their advocate in the community. This was not always easy because prejudice was high at the time.

I had arrived in Detroit just a few months after the race riots at the Sojourner Truth housing project in 1943, the worst such incident to take place during the war. Detroit was a tense place. The already brittle ethnic mosaic which included many ethnic groups from central and eastern Europe (prominent among whom were the Poles of the then township of Hamtramck) was suddenly hit by tens of thousands of in-migrants lured by the high pay of the war industries. Among them were large numbers of both blacks from the Deep South and whites: hillbillies from Kentucky and Tennessee and rednecks from the Piedmont. This was a prescription for disaster and, sure enough, disaster struck at the Sojourner Truth housing project, one of the frontiers of racial contact and conflict. When I arrived in Detroit, the aftershocks of the great riot were still reverberating.

For the first time I became personally aware of a phe-

26

nomenon by now a commonplace to students of race relations: the prejudice of minority groups toward each other. It was not so much the employers as the workers who objected to the Japanese-Americans. Before placing someone in a factory or office, we had to lay the groundwork carefully by persuading the workers to give him a chance. Many employers were quite willing to take Japanese labor, "but *you* convince the workers and the unions first," they would say. The greatest difficulty came from Poles and blacks. When I had to persuade a hostile Polish or black work force, I used to take an officer from the United Automobile Workers Union with me, white if the majority was Polish, black if it was black. Even with these precautions, there was one time when we had to be escorted ignominiously out of the plant under guard to escape a menacing encirclement of black workers who threatened to kill any "goddamn Jap" who showed up there, and looked quite willing to take the two of us as handy substitutes until something better came along.

Being thrown together so closely with people of Japanese descent for the first time, I was fascinated—the soft, almost cooing voices of the Nisei secretaries, the unpronounceable names, the alternately liquid and staccato flow of the language, the completely different human experiences, their almost palpable ties to remote islands and villages with exotic names.

I did not always like them. Once, after a lot of hard work, I located a position as an accountant for one young man who had been desperate to leave the camp but did not want to work in a factory. In the labor-short Detroit area, Japanese were primarily welcome as factory or farm hands. White-collar jobs—just as housing in decent, middle-class neighborhoods—were hard to come by, and when I succeeded I counted this as a more important step toward community acceptance than common-labor jobs. The young man in question received the same pay as white accountants in that particular small firm, and his employer was so sympathetic to his plight as a Japanese-American that he had even offered to take him into his home

27

until such time as he could find a place of his own. After about two weeks on the job, the young man showed up at my office with a sour look on his face and asked me to find him another job, and an accountant job at that. I was furious: these jobs were hard to get; the pay was good; in fact I considered it a major breakthrough. "What's wrong?" I asked. "You didn't tell me they were Jews," he said accusingly. "I can't work for a bunch of dirty Jews."

This happened several more times—delicate, sweet-faced Nisei girls quitting their jobs as maids in Jewish homes or stores, until I finally took advantage of an invitation to deliver a sermon in a Japanese Christian church on the psychology of prejudice among minority groups. With the Poles looking down on the blacks, the blacks on the Japanese, and the Japanese on the Jews, Detroit was a caricature of Tom Lehrer's "National Brotherhood Week":

> Oh, the Protestants hate the Catholics,
> And the Catholics hate the Protestants,
> And the Hindus hate the Moslems,
> And everybody hates the Jews.

It was not a lovable place.

But what struck me even more was not the prejudice from the outside, which I had after all expected, but the prejudice I found among Japanese-Americans themselves. One of the young men who had come to Detroit from the Tule Lake relocation camp was from a farm family in California. About twenty-eight years old, he was unself-consciously handsome and unfailingly affable. I had found a job for him in a war factory and, because of his gratitude—one of my first experiences of the excessiveness of Japanese gratitude—he often visited me. Japanese was his first language and he did not express himself well in English, but I felt drawn to him because he was always trying so hard to be friendly. There was something sad about his handsome smile, as if he had some deep wound from which he was slowly dying.

28

In fact, he did, as I later learned, thereby coming to understand a great deal about Japan. Takeo, as I shall call him here, had until the evacuation lived in a farm community that was largely inhabited by Japanese-Americans. Several years before the war broke out, he had fallen in love with one of the neighborhood girls. When he raised the subject of marriage to his parents, they went into a rage. Under no circumstances would they let him marry her because, it turned out, she was from an "untouchable" family. This traditional status, despite having been legally abolished in 1871, still remained alive both in Japan itself and among at least some Japanese-American immigrants. Her family lived as virtual pariahs in this little closed-in Japanese-American community, in spite of the fact that they were quite respectable, moderately successful farmers, and the girl herself had been a good student and eventually went through a teachers' training college.

The evacuation from the West Coast had separated Takeo and his love, and he was hoping I would find her a job so she could join him in Detroit. Would he then get married, I asked him? Oh no, he replied, his family wouldn't permit it. "Why don't you just go ahead and marry her? After all, you're not a child. You're a grown man of twenty-eight."

"That's out of the question," he replied. "You just can't do that in a Japanese family. It would break everyone's heart, and I would be written off the family register." All of this was new to me, fascinating grist for my anthropological mill.

About three months later, he became very ill, showing strange symptoms of occasional disorientation, fainting, and severe headaches. I finally managed to get him to a doctor, one our office frequently called on, and the doctor immediately put him into the hospital. The diagnosis came as a shock. He had a brain tumor that required immediate surgery. The prospects were not encouraging, so, at his request, I contacted his parents, still in the relocation camp, and they immediately came to Detroit, bringing along a daughter who spoke English well.

I was not privy to all that happened, but I later learned that Takeo had begged his parents, as a deathbed request, to let him marry his girl. Under these extreme circumstances, they relented, and the girl flew immediately to Detroit and was married to him in a civil ceremony at his bedside in the hospital. The next day, in a state of bliss, he went under the knife.

The story has a happy ending: the operation was successful. Takeo awoke to find himself both alive and married to the girl he loved. It was one of those rare Walter Mitty experiences: a dream fulfilled. But that Takeo should have had to go right to the brink of death to win his parents' approval taught me two important things about Japan: first, that parental authority was an awesome thing; and second, that Japan had its own problems of minorities and prejudice.

Being an anthropologist, I was naturally interested in learning something about the Japanese language. Surrounded by so many Japanese-Americans, one would expect this to be easy. But it was not. Most of the Nisei knew little or no Japanese, and even if they did it was to their advantage to pretend they did not. American society has often been a brutal homogenizer. It has an extraordinary capacity for making the second generation ashamed of its immigrant elders. To become American, the second generation must turn its back on the past, painstakingly unlearn the foreign accents of its homes, give up exotic ancestral tastes, and settle for the bland hamburger and milk.

This, it turned out, was as true of the second-generation Japanese as of the Poles, Jews, Italians, and Slovaks I had known in my native Chicago. But with the Nisei, the relocation experience intensified it: tradition, the old-country tie, was not only the visible mark of the despised past that made them different from others, it was also traitorous, the cause of the desperate pariah condition in which they found themselves. The official regulations made this even more explicit: one of the criteria for clearance was how "Japanese" they were, and the indices of "Japaneseness" were: previous attendance in Japanese language schools; degree of speaking and writing ability in

30

Japanese; interest in traditional cultural activities (flower arrangement, judo, the military arts, Japanese music, etc.). Ability to speak Japanese well, and particularly to read it, was *prima facie* evidence of unreliability. My poor relocatees were not about to raise doubts about their loyalty by allowing me, an official representative of government, to believe that they knew Japanese well enough to teach it.

It was at this point that, walking down the streets of downtown Detroit one day, I ran into a college buddy. William Mulloy was already an experienced archaeologist, and today he is a famous professor (University of Wyoming) who, among other things, is known for his scientific work on Thor Heyerdahl's expeditions. But at that time he was a first lieutenant in the United States Army. Bill, it turned out, as we unwound a bit over beer in the Pontchartrain Cellars restaurant, was acting commanding officer of the Army Intensive Japanese Language School at the University of Michigan.

"Why don't you volunteer for it?" he proposed, when I told him of my interest in the language. And that is how I got started. I applied both for the army school in Ann Arbor and the corresponding navy school at the University of Colorado.

I was accepted by both, but this immediately confronted me with a difficult moral problem. On a straight choice in terms of personal benefit, the navy was clearly preferable. Whether it was better academically than the army program, I do not know; it was certainly not inferior. But the navy program was for fourteen months, while the army's was for eighteen months (not counting two months of military training). What was more important was that the navy treated its language students like officers. At the end of the first three months of training, they were commissioned as ensigns. This meant that they went through most of their training as "officers and gentlemen," as the old phrase has it. But in the army language school, the students were commissioned as second lieutenants only at the end of the full eighteen months. Except for those who already had attained some military rank before entering the school, the students all spent their first fourteen months as privates, first class, and then, after completing basic training, were promoted to the T-5 (technician, fifth grade) rank of corporal. It was obvious that the navy program was gentlemanly and comfortable, that the pay was much better than the army's, and that one could study in an altogether more civilized environment. An army private's pay was then $21 per month. Additional allowances were paid for family and children, but this went directly to the family. As a naval ensign, with officer's pay and allowances, I would have been able to maintain a home with my wife and child. As an army PFC, I would have to put my wife to work.

Clearly, then, the navy offered a better deal from any point of view. But having been an officer of the War Relocation Authority and having been closely involved in the Japanese-American problem, I was keenly aware of the fact that the navy would not accept Japanese-Americans in service. Altogether, the navy's record on race was much worse than the army's: blacks were used only in hard labor and menial positions and Orientals only in steward, kitchen, and other lowly service positions.

The army, however, after the initial shock of the relocation had worn off, had a much better record. Although it still retained lingering suspicions about the loyalty of the Japanese-Americans, it did accept them and it even commissioned a few. Before the war was over, the highest-ranking Japanese-American, John Aiso—who was the first academic director of the Military Intelligence Service Language School (MISLS)—reached the rank of lieutenant colonel. (He crowned his career as a justice on the California high court, from which he only recently retired.) Army attitudes were gradually influenced by the outstanding combat record of the two all-Japanese-American outfits, the 442d Regimental Combat Team from Hawaii and the 100th Batallion, perhaps the most decorated units in the United States Army. They had just covered themselves with glory in the Italian campaign and then later in

32

the Normandy fighting, and the army was increasingly willing to give them a chance. I was therefore in the position of morally and politically favoring the army but preferring the navy for reasons of practical benefit to myself.

My private wrestling with this moral dilemma had no witnesses. I was the only one who cared. And when I finally made my moral gesture to posterity and accepted the army offer, it was with the hollow feeling that the gesture was in vain, a "sweetness wasted on the desert air." Nobody could care less, certainly not the Japanese-Americans I had been looking after in Detroit, or my friends and relatives who would only think I was crazy to throw away the chance for a quick commission. The die was cast and there was no turning back, but often, later on, when I was in another of my financial crises or when I was being humiliated by some noncom or officer flaunting his petty authority, I was sure that I had made the wrong choice.

II ✩

COMPANY A

Fort Sheridan

It was on a sunny but coolish day in April 1944 that I packed my wife and one-and-a-half-year-old son into our 1939 Ford V-8 and set out for the army induction center at Fort Sheridan, Illinois. Chicago's wealthy North Shore suburbs rolled by one after another, each a further reminder that this graciousness was no longer to be part of my life for the next several years.

Fort Sheridan had been a fixed point in my consciousness ever since my childhood days. It was a well-known landmark, and several of the uncles on my father's side of the family had touched base there during their military service in World War I. Sitting in the midst of Chicago's elegant northern suburbs, it looked more like a golf club or a country club than like the forbidding military fortress the word "fort" conjures up. The two uncles on my mother's side sometimes played golf in country clubs nearby the fort, and on the few occasions that I visited them there I was always aware of the fort's looming presence. From the road one saw whitewashed Mediterranean-style bungalows and sporty-looking young men going about their normal lives. A less military scene it would be hard to imagine.

Kissing my wife and child goodbye, I handed over the car keys, gave some ritual husbandly and fatherly advice, and then went inside Fort Sheridan for the first time in my life. Reality quickly crowded in. Hundreds of young men just like myself arriving for their induction into the army, nervously milled around. After a brief introductory orientation lecture, we were divided into squads, each in the charge of a veteran army non-com, and under his cynically expert guidance went through the preliminary induction steps—medical examinations, psychiatric interviews, AGST (Army General Standard Test), aptitude tests, orientation and training movies, haircuts, making beds, and doing KP.

At the end of that first day, on my way back to the barracks to which I had been assigned, I found myself walking along with a young chap, slightly younger than myself, who seemed to be both fastidious and ill at ease. After some rough handling by army types and semiliterate sergeants, I knew how he felt. All day long I had been kicking myself for the foolish—and useless—moral pride that had made me go into the army rather than the navy. My casual walking companion, it turned out, was a Ph.D. candidate in English literature at the University of Wisconsin working on a dissertation on "Dickens and His Times." The Sheridan cadres, he felt, took special pleasure in tormenting intellectuals like himself. An engineering or a law major had a salable skill that received at least grudging respect. But a literature major? Not a chance.

I congratulated myself secretly that I had had the foresight to enter the army equipped with orders for the Japanese language school, thus sparing myself the agony my newly made Wisconsin friend was going through. An English major was bad enough, but eventually there might be a place for him in training, I and E (Information and Education), public relations, or administration. But an anthropologist? That night there were not many of the twenty of us in that barracks who slept well.

From our second day, while awaiting the results of the sundry tests and the processing of our orders, we were assigned to various tasks. My assignment was to the unit headquarters office because, it appeared, I had done extremely well in the typing test. The minimum army standard for classification as a typist was, I believe, thirty words per minute. I had done seventy to eighty. "Congratulations," the sergeant in charge of the office, a gray, mousy little man, who looked as if he had spent all of his life in dusty files or in library stacks, said to me. "You are going to be a clerk-typist."

"Oh no, I'm not," I replied, suddenly appalled. "I have my orders for the Japanese language school."

"That's all right," the sergeant consoled me, "we can have them changed."

"Over my dead body!" I screamed.

Several days after I had gotten over my fright about the clerk-typist assignment, I finally received travel orders. I was instructed to report to troop train such-and-such for transfer to my permanent station. I packed my single duffel bag, which was all we were allowed to carry, and presented myself for transport to the train station. After all of our rush to get there, it was the proverbial army "hurry up and wait."

We were delayed for several hours, and during that time I talked to some of the men around me. All of them, it turned out, were being assigned to military-police training. Was I being sent to the wrong place, I began to wonder, and so I searched out the sergeant in charge and asked him where my orders were taking me. "Troop transport destinations are a military secret," he told me, and this answer only increased my uneasiness. I then found a second lieutenant, who looked as if he might be civilized (in those days that meant, as far as I was concerned, a university graduate), and explained my position to him. He looked at my orders. "You're on your way to MP training camp," he said, with which the panic button went off.

I whipped out my copy of my original orders, the orders on the basis of which I had enlisted in the army. The lieutenant read them through and said, "You'd better get moving. This train is going to be taking off soon." I ran to the transport head-quarters and demanded that they do something immediately to straighten out the mistake in my orders. This required them to call back to the fort, find the officer in charge, and then wait for the results of the inquiry. All of this took about half an hour, and my duffel bag was somewhere in the luggage compartment of the train and it was impossible to get it out on time.

As the train pulled out of the station, I was very happy to be still there on the platform, saved from a fate worse than death; but my baggage went off by itself. When I arrived at the University of Michigan to report for language school, I was still wearing the same clothes I had been wearing on the train platform. My luggage finally reached me in Ann Arbor much later.

Arrival

I had escaped the Scylla of clerk-typing and the Charybdis of MP training. But what lay ahead? The first encounter with my new army post was heartwarming. A beautiful spring day, and I was in a university, not an army barracks. Company A of the AIJLS (Army Intensive Japanese Language School), also called the AJLS (Army Japanese Language School), occupied the quadrangle formed by Hillsdale and Tyler dormitories at the University of Michigan, and even though everybody was in khaki, the academic mark was unmistakable. In contrast with the strident and assertively know-nothing voices at Fort Sheridan, suddenly there were restrained, cultivated voices with educated accents.

Company A was a part of the MISLS (Military Intelligence Service Language School), then headquartered in Camp Savage, Minnesota. Shortly after my entry into the army, the language school headquarters transferred to Fort Snelling, Minnesota. In Minnesota, Japanese-Americans received language and combat intelligence training. Toward the end of the war, a few classes in Chinese and Korean were added, but the school's main mission was to train Japanese language speakers. The mission of my school, the AIJLS, was to train Caucasian and other non-Japanese U.S. citizens (we had one Chinese and one Filipino in our company). It was estimated that the non-Japanese required a year of intensive preparation to reach the Nisei level, after which they were to join the others in Minnesota for advanced language training.

Our Company A at Michigan was distinguished from the Savage and Snelling contingents not only by being entirely non-Japanese but also by having the status of an officer candidate school. Upon the successful completion of the training, Company A men became second lieutenants; the Nisei remained enlisted men.

Although the AIJLS was a military organization, it was conducted by civilians under contract with the University of Michigan and housed there. Professor Joseph Yamagiwa, the head of the university's Japanese language department, was the academic head of the program, and under him there were, at its high point, more than fifty faculty members, all Japanese-Americans.

English in Wartime Japan

It is instructive to contrast for a moment the fate of English in wartime Japan and of Japanese in the United States. In Japan, English was looked upon as a dangerous, corrupting influence, and it was discouraged. In the United States, however, the war raised the study of Japanese to entirely new levels.

In Japan, it was recognized, of course, that English was important for military intelligence, propaganda, and international contacts, but this recognition came with reluctance, particularly among the more nationalistic elements. When you hate the monk, you hate even his clothes, an old Japanese proverb runs, and official Japanese attitudes exemplified the proverb.

"Because it is spoken by Japan's enemy nations," the *Japan Times and Advertiser* of March 4, 1942, wrote, "the English language has fallen into discredit and there is even an outcry for its abolition." Thus had the wheel come full turn. In 1872, Arinori Mori, Japan's first diplomatic representative to the

United States, and later its first Minister of Education, had proposed a drastic thesis for the newly developing nation: "Abolish Japanese, Adopt English." In World War II reactionary promilitarists reversed the terms of this thesis and called the country to "Abolish English, Adopt Japanese."

During the early part of the war, the attack on English and on "decadent" Western culture was pressed vigorously. There were no specific laws or ordinances ordering this, so far as I can determine, but administrative guidance plus the changed attitudes toward the West were sufficient. The Eighth Section of the Army Chief of Staff Headquarters, which was in charge of information, held frequent briefings with the radio and the press, and at these put forward the army's position on the "purification" of the language.

It must be kept in mind that the Japanese language, since the mid-1880s, has been penetrated by thousands, even tens of thousands, of European words, usually by way of English. These words, dealing with modern science and technology or aspects of modern living, have become so domesticated in Japan that they now form part of the language stock of all people, at every level of society. "We had briefings every week or so," a newspaperman who used to take part in these conferences told me. "The major who usually did the briefings was himself a moderate, and he tried to present the headquarters' position as reasonably as possible." The army was particularly sensitive about the radio because the spoken language had such immediate impact. The word "news" (pronounced *nyūsu* in Japanese) became *hōdō* and "announcer" (*anaunsa*) became *hōsōin*. But "radio" remained radio (although pronounced *rajio*) on the rationale that the word was Latin in origin, not English.

The area of mass culture, where almost all of the basic vocabulary was imported, took some of the heaviest blows. "Baseball" (pronounced *beisubōru*) became *yakyū*, "basketball" (*basuketto-bōru*) became *rōkyū*, and "tennis" (*tenisu*) *teikyū*. Japanese words had to be used for all technical baseball terms: "out" (*au-to*) became *damé*, "strike" (*sutoraiki*) became *yoshi*, "strikeout" (*sutoraiki au-to*) became *sanshin*. Finally in April 1943, the Ministry of Education banned baseball entirely. The automobile culture, today a veritable bastion of foreignisms, reverted to labored Japanese, using words that contemporary Japanese people would be hard put today to recognize.

But English was too deeply entrenched in Japan's modernization to be so readily dislodged. Schools discouraged English and often cut down the number of hours devoted to it; some even cut it out entirely. But it remained a required subject for middle school students intending to go on to university and for high school students in the so-called "A Course." The alternative at high school, however, the "B Course," which required German, rather than English, expanded considerably.

If English could not be rooted out of the school system, it was placed under tighter control. English language textbooks were revised and made uniform. Japanese context, as well as substance, in tune with wartime policy was introduced. Tom and Mary were replaced by Tarō and Hanako; going to the ball game on Sunday was replaced by going to the factory or to the farms to help the hardworking farmers. "On Wednesdays we wrote letters to soldiers" replaced "On Wednesdays we wrote letters to our friends."

American-born Nisei living in Japan were especially sensitive to the problem. Some found that knowing English gave them an advantage, since this knowledge was useful for the war effort. Others found that it brought them under suspicion of disloyalty. Ironically, had they been in the United States when the war broke out, they might have found themselves suspected of disloyalty for knowing Japanese, like so many of my charges at the War Relocation Authority. One Nisei I knew told of one of his friends being beaten up in front of the Tokyo Central Railroad Station for reading a copy of the English-language *Nippon Times*.

The abolition of English was easier to contemplate in the Japanese army, many of whose younger officers had come under the influence of ultranationalist ideologues. But it was not so easy for the navy, whose entire tradition was English. Even before Japan started to modernize in a serious way, after the Meiji Restoration of 1868, the feudal principality of Chōshū, which had played a leading role in the Restoration movement, dominated the new army. But the Satsuma domain dominated the modern navy. In August of 1863, Satsuma had been bombarded into defeat by English naval guns in the brief Anglo-Satsuma War. But this experience, far from making Satsuma hostile to England, turned it into a great admirer of the British navy.

Munenori Terajima was at that time physician to the lord of Satsuma, Nariakira Shimazu, and a "naval expert" in those days. He was captured by the British during the bombardment of the city of Kagoshima and, as someone has described it, he walked "into the jaws of the lion [and] emerged thoroughly impressed with the sharpness of the teeth." He thereupon became the joint supervisor of the party of samurai students that Satsuma sent to England in 1865, of which Arinori Mori (already mentioned in connection with the "Abolish Japanese" thesis) was the most famous member. Although each of the students was assigned a separate subject, naval warfare was not an unimportant one, and when, after the Restoration, the modern Imperial Japanese Navy was established, the English tradition was well entrenched. For many years English was the language of instruction in the Naval Academy and, while in the 1930s army officers seemed to be inspired by Germany, naval officers continued to look to England.

English was so deeply rooted that it was not only part of the professional vocabulary of the navy but also of its innermost argot. A former wartime naval officer, Tsutomu Aoki, lists some delightful examples of English "made in Japan" in common use during the war. *Inchi*, for example was a girlfriend, or someone with whom one was intimate—from the English "intimate," pronounced *inchimeito* by Japanese. The commanding officer of a vessel was called the *keppu*, from the English "captain," which became *kyaputan* which became *kyappu* and then *keppu*.

A girl was a *kōperu*, from the English word "copper"; the reason is that the English word "daughter" is mispronounced as *dōtā* by the Japanese and the first syllable, the *dō* of *dōtā*, is assigned the Chinese character 銅, which happens to mean "copper", and this in Japanese mispronunciation becomes *kōperu*. "Scale" (pronounced *sukēru*) was a waitress. How? There is an old Japanese word, *shaku-fu*, which means waitress. The Chinese character for *shaku* is 酌. The right side of the character (勺) taken by itself means "scale." Pronounce it Japanese-style, and there you have it. The madam of a Japanese-style inn was called "god" (pronounced *goddo*), not so much because of her exalted status, but rather through the following sequence: the madam is called *kami-san* in Japanese; *kami* means "head" or "chief," but it also means "god" (just as we use the word "lord" for both the lord of the manor and the Lord, our God); translate this into English, mispronounce Japanese-style, and you have "god."

Therefore, if young officers during the war sat at mess or in their clubs discussing the relative merits of "S-play with a black as against being long with a white girl," it is unlikely that the enlisted men serving their dinner or their drinks would understand what they were talking about. Nor would an English speaker, in spite of the fact that the words used are English. In the first place, they are mispronounced in such a way that he would be hard put to recognize them: *esu-purei* (S-play), *burakku* (black), *rongu* (long), *waito* (white), and *kōperu* (copper, for daughter, or girl). But even if he somehow could figure all of this out, he would still not understand because the S of S-play refers to a "singer," that is, a geisha or a professional entertainer, and therefore S-play means "playing around with a geisha." And the "black" and "white" do not refer to race, or color: in Japanese usage, a professional is "black" and an amateur is "white." "Long" again refers not to a physical attribute but means "being attracted to," a direct translation from a Japanese phrase "the tip of the nose is long." In other words, the issue is not whether one should go for a black or for a white girl but rather whether one should take up with a professional, a geisha, or get involved with a local girl.

Loan words were so deeply entrenched in the Japanese language that even with the kind of radical surgery performed on baseball, it could not be entirely excised. A leading journalist of the period tells the story of the spokesman of the army's Information Headquarters having to use an English word to explain army policy on loan words. "We would like you to use Japanese as much as possible, rather than English. But if you overdo it, you might very well *spoil* what you want to say." Everything in the preceding sentence was in Japanese except the English word "spoil." Although this is not exactly a standard usage in English, it is understandable; more important, it was the only word the army officer could think of to express what he wanted to say.

The crowning irony was the Greater East Asia Conference in Tokyo in December 1943. The very symbol of Japan's driving the decadent Western imperialist influence out of Asia, it had to be conducted in English. "It is strange that the Greater East Asia Conference is conducted in the language of the enemy," wrote the famous journalist Kiyoshi Kiyozawa. "I hear that Tōjō, too, is upset by this."

Japanese in Prewar America

In the United States, however, the trend was the exact opposite. But before we pat ourselves on the back, it is salutary to recall that the base for the study of Japanese in the United States was much narrower than the base in Japan for the study of English. In Japan, English was an important school subject, even at the middle school level, and for university entrance it was virtually mandatory; in the United States, it was offered at only a small number of universities. At the beginning of the war, apart from Americans of Japanese ancestry, only a handful of Americans could handle the Japanese language in any reasonable degree, probably less than one hundred. The distinguished authority on Japanese literature, Donald Keene, in his memoirs, *Meeting with Japan*, writes that he had heard there were only fifty, and "Although my knowledge of Japanese was primitive, I wondered if I might be one of the fifty."

The question naturally arises as to why the Japanese drew in their horns on English during the war, choosing to look upon it as a dangerous corrupting influence, while we took exactly the opposite course and plunged into the study of the enemy language with gusto. When I first went to Korea after the war, many of my Korean friends were resentful that the only Asian language American soldiers seemed to know was Japanese. How come none of us could speak Korean? "Japan was our enemy," I would explain, "so we had to learn Japanese in order to fight them. Korea was our friend, so we did not feel any necessity to learn Korean." This is, I still honestly believe, the truth—whether the view itself that it was not necessary to learn Korean was correct or not. Korean only came to be taught in the army language school in 1945, as the war was coming down the home stretch and it was becoming increasingly clear that we would have some role in Korea and therefore needed some Korean language capability. But my Korean friends never quite believed my explanation, always suspecting that it concealed a preference for Japan. In any event, as far as Japanese was concerned, it was during the war that it saw its first historic period of flowering in the United States.

There was, on the American side, a combination of motives. The first was simple pragmatic necessity. The existing Japanese language capacity in the United States, even if the Japanese-Americans were included, was inadequate to the needs of the war. Codes had to be broken, signals analyzed, propaganda countered, military operations diagnosed, economic and political trends monitored, and eventually—if everything went as Americans were supremely confident it would—prisoners would have to be handled, troops called upon to surrender, and negotiations conducted.

But these eminently practical needs were not all. There was also a feeling that our long stretch of smug isolation, during which we had been inattentive to the vast movements going on in the world, had much to do with our failure to understand the situation and our slowness in responding appropriately. It was as if the collective ears of America, which until then had only been tuned in on domestic affairs, were suddenly opened to the world. The shift of the collective American rabbit-ears antennae outward brought in new sounds, new thoughts, new ideas, and new experiences. And the newness was itself exciting to many people.

In any event, whether the number of American speakers of Japanese was fifty or one hundred by the time the Pacific War broke out, there were very few of them. They consisted primarily of three groups. First, the language officers trained by the army, navy, and foreign service. These were very carefully selected men assigned to study Japanese at first for two, and then later for three, years in Japan. During their period of study they were required to live for one year outside of the major urban centers in order to deepen their contact with ordinary Japanese people and their knowledge of Japanese life. At the end of the period, the officer was usually assigned as attaché to the embassy or, hopefully, to some work in the United States that made use of his language training. The program was informal. There were no formal classes, only private tutors. All that was expected of the language officers was that at the end of their two or three years they emerge as competent speakers of Japanese. Admiral Ellis Zacharias, one of the most famous of the language officers, felt strongly that this casualness was not a good thing but rather a reflection of the military's failure to appreciate the importance of intelligence as a military function; therefore it did not give language training and professional intelligence work the attention they deserved.

But as war with Japan began to appear more likely, several of these prewar language officers took the lead in establishing the wartime language schools. During the 1930s, Naoe Naganuma, the head of a language school in Tokyo, came in charge of the tutors of the language officers. (His school is still in existence.)

Since no systematic and advanced Japanese language training materials existed in the United States (the universities concentrated primarily on the written language) when the military language schools started, the Naganuma readers brought back by the language officers became the basis for the development of the wartime curriculum. Both the army and the navy programs consisted basically of the Naganuma graded readers plus additional materials that were worked up on an *ad hoc* basis by the instructors during the course of the war.

The prewar language officer program produced some outstanding graduates, including General Maxwell Taylor, Admiral Ellis Zacharias, and foreign service officers U. Alexis Johnson, John Emmerson, and Marshall Green. But there were very few of them. By the time of the outbreak of the Pacific War, the navy had trained forty-two Japanese language officers (and sixteen Chinese language officers), and the army about the same number.

To us in the wartime schools, struggling—at least in the army—on enlisted man's pay and suffering daily indignities from our superiors, the life of the prewar language officers sounded like heaven itself. The reports we heard about the life they had led and the gentlemanly conditions under which they had studied were in dramatic contrast to the conditions in which we found ourselves. Particularly mouth-watering were the tales of their mandatory year in the provinces, living and learning without fixed program or duties. The language officer who surfaced after his year in the provinces speaking "feminine language" was a stock character in our pantheon of the prewar golden age of the language officer. Speaking feminine language did not, in that day, suggest homosexuality to us, but rather that the officer had lived with a Japanese girl during the year and that he had spent his time with her rather than mixing with all and sundry as he was supposed to do. "Pillow talk," we called this, punning on the Japanese term *makura kotoba*, which can be so translated literally, but which in fact refers to fixed epithets, or descriptive words used in Japanese poetry, plays, or declamations. And it was our most ardent hope to find ourselves in a similar situation one day.

The second major group of American speakers of Japanese consisted of the so-called BIJs, or those who were "born in Japan." Usually they were the children of missionary families, although an occasional business family might be found among them. Professor Edwin O. Reischauer, Harvard, and Professor Otis Cary, of Dōshisha University in Kyoto, are distinguished examples of this genre. Reischauer—our ambassador to Japan from 1961 to 1965—was born of missionary parents and raised in Japan. Although he attended English language schools, he acquired through his early experience a profound personal feeling for Japan. Cary was born in Kyoto of a missionary family associated with Dōshisha University. Dōshisha had been founded in 1875 as a Christian English-language school by Jō Niijima, an early graduate of Amherst College, and was finally recognized as a university only in 1912. The Dōshisha–Amherst connection thus formed has remained to the present time. Cary attended Japanese primary school for some years, becoming therewith almost completely fluent in Japanese, and then high school and university in the United States. During the war he went to the navy language school, and after the war he returned to make his home in Japan, back at Dōshisha once again, where as professor of history and director of Amherst House, he carries on the family tradition.

The third group that provided some Japanese-speaking U.S. citizens consisted of businessmen and students who, through some accident of personal history, had spent a significant stretch of time in Japan or had studied Japanese in American universities. Thomas Blakemore, today the senior American lawyer in Japan, was one of these. Before the war, he was sent to study Japanese law by the Crane Foundation (which is no longer in existence). He came back to the United States to become the only American authority on Japanese law at that time. During the war he served in the navy, and during the Occupation he played an important role in the reform of Japan's

48

civil, criminal, and commercial codes as a staff member of GHQ's Legal Section.

Altogether, however, the number of Americans not of Japanese descent who could use the Japanese language at a literate level was very small indeed. Clearly a war with Japan required a much greater language capability than existed among Americans who were not of Japanese descent.

I have said except for Japanese Americans. Yet they, after all, constituted the greatest reserve of Japanese language capability in the United States. There were, in 1942, some 260,000 in Hawaii and on the mainland—mostly in California. Why were they not sufficient for the needs of the country? The basic reason was quite simple. As Brigadier General John Weckerling, one of the founders of the Army Intensive Japanese Language School, wrote many years later: "The treacherous attack on Pearl Harbor naturally engendered [a] great hatred of the Japanese, and as a corollary the public and the army as a whole regarded the loyalty of all Japanese-Americans at that time as doubtful." This feeling went so far that soon after the start of the war, orders were issued that no Nisei were to serve overseas. It was only later in the war that this regulation was relaxed and the army trained Japanese-Americans for overseas combat. But even then, most of them were in segregated units.

By an odd irony of fate, it turned out that the establishment of segregated units for the Nisei may very well have advanced their integration and acceptance into American life more effectively than "democratic" integration into military units would have. The two Nisei combat units, which were deliberately kept away from the Pacific in order to avoid the possibility of a conflict of loyalties, were active in the European theater, and the very fact that they were highly visible as Japanese-Americans made their brilliant military achievements and their valor all the more conspicuous. There may have been some farsighted officers who anticipated this outcome, but it was more likely the result of unplanned and happy accident.

The language officer program in Japan had come to an end in

1940 as a result of the growing tension between the United States and Japan. But within the United States only a handful of universities taught Japanese, and this was to a small number of students and at a leisurely pace.

Since the language needs far exceeded the existing capacity, the armed forces started a crash program on a large scale. There were three major institutions: the Navy Japanese Language School, which, by the end of the war, trained about one thousand two hundred and fifty language officers; the army's MISLS (Military Intelligence Service Language School), which trained about seven thousand (six thousand Nisei and seven hundred and eighty Caucasian or other U.S. citizens of non-Japanese descent); and the army's ASTP (Army Specialized Training Program), which provided elementary training for over fifteen thousand enlisted men in a half dozen different schools. In addition to these major programs, another thousand or two were trained in miscellaneous programs in civil affairs, military government, and the Signal Corps.

The Wartime Language Schools

After the closedown of the overseas language officer program in 1940, the armed forces did not resume formal training programs until 1941. The navy started a school in June 1941, at the University of California at Berkeley, and then opened a second school at Harvard directed by Professor Reischauer. The Harvard program closed down in 1942, but the program started at Berkeley continued to the very end of the war. But not in Berkeley: in 1942 it moved to the University of Colorado in Boulder, Colorado. The reason for the move was embedded in the irony of the times. The navy would not accept Japanese-Americans as students, but it needed them as teachers. But since the teachers, even though the navy needed them, were required by law to be evacuated from the West Coast, the navy language school was forced to move, too. The Boulder facilities became overstrained, and in mid-1945 the navy opened an additional school on the campus of the Oklahoma Agricultural

50

and Mechanical College (now Oklahoma State University) in Stillwater, Oklahoma.

The army started its program a little later in the year, November 1941. But because of the successful advocacy of Kai Rasmussen (later colonel and commandant of the school), Brigadier General Weckerling, and other ex-language officers, the army was persuaded to take a chance on using Nisei for military language work. However, a deep distrust continued to prevail, and they were to be placed under strict control. It was therefore decided to train Caucasians (plus other non-Japanese U.S. citizens) to take charge of Nisei language teams—eventually in the ratio of one Caucasian officer to ten enlisted men. One of the Caucasians in the very first Camp Savage class described his training as follows: "We were told that our principal mission was to learn sufficient Japanese so that we could be sure the Nisei were translating, interrogating, and reporting accurately, and not deceiving our intelligence people with false information . . . that is what we were trained to detect." In the Pacific combat areas, navy language officers were also assigned Nisei language teams to work with.

The first army class started in November 1941 in a converted hangar at Crissey Field in the Presidio of San Francisco with sixty students—fifty-eight Nisei and two Caucasians who had some background in Japanese—and five instructors.

The original expectation had been that since the Nisei had a background in the language, all that would be necessary was a few weeks of intensive language training to polish up their Japanese, give them specialized military vocabulary, and prepare them for combat intelligence. This expectation turned out to be entirely incorrect. The overwhelming majority of the Nisei seemed to be far more backward in Japanese than anyone had suspected. In preparation for the establishment of the language school in the Presidio, Kai Rasmussen tested three thousand seven hundred enlisted Japanese-Americans, using the Naganuma readers as test materials. He found only 3 percent of them "accomplished linguists," 4 percent "proficient," and 3 percent "useful only after a considerable period of training." How much this reflected the true state of their Japanese language ability and how much is to be attributed to something else—their fear of being considered un-American if they knew Japanese too well, or their unwillingness to be used in the war against Japan, or the difficulty of judging the language ability of immigrants from written tests—it would be hard to say.

A month after the program was launched, the attack on Pearl Harbor came, and with it the evacuation of the Japanese-Americans from the West Coast states. The army, like the navy, had to move its language school out of California in order to retain the Japanese-American teachers. In May 1942 the army school moved to Camp Savage, Minnesota. Savage was selected not only because it had the space necessary for the planned expansion of the school but also because Colonel Rasmussen, who was made commandant in May, was himself of Danish descent, and he felt that the Scandinavian immigrant stock in the state of Minnesota was likely to be more tolerant of the Japanese-Americans than the citizens of most other states. In this, he proved to be right. Within two years, the school outgrew its facilities in Camp Savage, and in August 1944 it was transferred to more ample quarters in Fort Snelling.

In the first few classes at Camp Savage, Caucasian students were mixed with the Nisei, even though upon graduation they would become officers and their fellow Nisei students remain enlisted men. The first Savage class, for example, included thirty Caucasians along with one hundred and forty-five Nisei. One of the Caucasians in that group was Faubion Bowers, who later became one of General MacArthur's aides. To the more pedestrian among us, he seemed to have reached the very pinnacle of possible achievement for a language officer. Later he married the Indian writer, Santha Rama Rau, who had lived in Japan for a while when her father, Sir Benegal Rau, was Indian ambassador, and then he went on to a distinguished career as a writer on cultural subjects and the arts.

But after a few of the mixed classes, it was decided that the non-Japanese-American students started from a point too far behind to be able to keep up with the Japanese-Americans. A separate school was therefore started for the Caucasians (and other non-Japanese) at the University of Michigan, in Ann Arbor. Although Ann Arbor was a bare thirty-five miles from central Detroit and even closer to the newly built wartime boom town of Willow Run, whence the newly built Ford Motor Company poured out tens of thousands of bombers for service on the different war fronts, it was at that time far removed from all of that, a gracious college town of tree-lined avenues.

Ann Arbor

On the surface, wartime Ann Arbor, Michigan, was a typical Midwestern university town with a light overlay of khaki. There were solid wood houses surrounded by stately lawns and gardens, and then, as one moved closer in to the campus, the inevitable crowding and seediness of the rooming houses interspersed with the pseudo-Florentine, pseudo-Norman, pseudo-antebellum Southern, and pseudo-old-brick fraternities and sororities. The campus was a series of parks and fine lawns with a mixture of styles reflecting the decade-by-decade change in American university architectural tastes. If one could have looked at it internally at that moment in late April 1944, one would have seen that there was a disproportionately large number of female students, a shortage of able-bodied male students, and a peculiar spottiness in the faculty that reflected the vagaries of the Selective Service System. One never knew who was going to be called up into service and who was not, who was physically fit and who was not, who was expendable and who was in a position requiring exemption from military service.

Like other American campuses during the war, the University of Michigan had devoted a significant percentage of its facilities to military or other governmental needs connected with the war. I cannot now remember all of the military training and research activities going on at the time, but in addition to my own Company A, there was an Army Specialized Training

53

Program in Japanese—conducted by Professor Yamagiwa and his staff—providing a year of training for enlisted men in conversation, but without the reading of Chinese characters; a civil affairs training program for officers which gave about six months of Japanese once-over-lightly; and a legal training program in the law school for the Judge Advocate-General Section of the army. Many years later I discovered that a doctor I once consulted in New York, who is professor at Cornell University's New York Hospital, took his medical training as an enlisted man in the army at the University of Michigan at the very same time that I was there. I did not at that time even know that there was such a program. And I would not be surprised to learn that there were many others.

Ours was the fourth class in the AIJLS at the University of Michigan. We started out as a company of about one hundred and sixty-five enlisted men and thirteen officer students. When we arrived in Ann Arbor in May 1944, the preceding company, with approximately the same composition, was still present. It had started six months before us and would remain until the end of the year, when it went on to its basic training, and after that to six months in Fort Snelling. The next class entered the school in January 1945.

We were billeted in a university dormitory consisting of two buildings, Hinsdale House and Tyler House. In principle, all of the enlisted men were required to live in the dormitories and the officer students allowed to live off-campus if they preferred.

We married students, whose families had come to Ann Arbor to be with us, were allowed to study evenings outside of supervised study hall if we maintained good grades, and to sleep at home, rather than in barracks, on weekends and holidays. Occasionally, either with special permission or as a kind of reward for good behavior, we were permitted to spend the night at home at other times as well. As soon as I was reasonably settled in Ann Arbor, my wife and son came, and we set out to find ourselves a place to live. Any place in Ann Arbor was too expensive for an enlisted man on enlisted man's pay and allowances, so unless one had an independent income, or was supported by generous parents or relatives, wives had to go to work. My wife, who was a psychologist, took a job in the Ann Arbor school system. Since rents were too much for us singly, we joined together with several other couples in a like position to rent a house. With several couples, not only would the cost be lower but the women could also share the babysitting and the household chores, thus making life easier for everybody.

The Cast of Characters: Us

At any given moment, therefore, there were over three hundred enlisted men and twenty-five officer students in the school. Our class was scheduled to spend one year at the University of Michigan, then two months in Fort McClelland, Alabama, for basic training, and finally six months along with the Nisei at Fort Snelling. At the end of that time, the enlisted men who had passed the course successfully would be commissioned and then sent on to their combat assignments. By our time, several classes had already gone into the field, and reports were filtering back about their experiences in the Gilberts, Guadalcanal, New Guinea, and, for the lucky ones, the sybaritic life in Australia or in Honolulu, headquarters of the JICPOA (Joint Intelligence Center, Pacific Ocean Area). By late summer 1944, the first Michigan class had hit the field, and many of them were eventually to end up in the Marianas, the Philippines, and Okinawa.

The selection process assured that the average quality of the student body would be high. For entry into the school, the students had to rank high in intelligence, at least as measured on the AGST (Army General Standard Test). The rumor was that an IQ of 130 was required, but whether that was in fact the cutoff point I have never been able to confirm. Nevertheless, the rumor itself was a fillip to the company pride. Even if it was not exactly true, it felt very good to believe that one belonged to a company in which the minimum IQ was 130. The second major requirement—again, with a tiny number of exceptions, including myself—was that the students have some previous experience of a significant character with the Japanese language. These included BIJs, the born-in-Japans who had lived there for a significant period, people who had studied Japanese in university, and the upper 10 percent of those who had completed the one-year ASTP programs. These stringent criteria made for a very high caliber of student indeed.

My roommate, for example, was still a student in the City College of New York, but in the very next room there were a professor of drama at the University of Hawaii and a former diplomat who had been stationed in Japan. Of the two men who had joined with me to rent a very large sorority house for our families, one was a law student from the West Coast. The other was the son of missionaries, born and raised in Japan. He had returned to the United States for his university education and then married, had a family, and settled into a social work career. (Eventually, he became head of a social work agency in Minneapolis and had nothing further to do with Japan.) Solis Horwitz (later one of the chief prosecutors in the International War Crimes Tribunals in Tokyo) was a lawyer and an assistant professor of law at the University of Pittsburgh. We had bankers, radio announcers, singers, reporters, a regional planning expert, the sons of a famous writer and of a famous orchestra conductor, and graduate students from many universities.

The BIJs were a diverse crew. Some of them were the children of missionaries, others of businessmen, journalists, and educators. Some of them had done some serious study of Japanese, even to the point of attending Japanese school; others had only the smattering that came from hearing Japanese spoken occasionally by servants or neighborhood children in the interstices of their English-language schedules at school and at home. In the country of the blind the one-eyed man is king, runs an old proverb, and for a while the BIJs were able to lord it over us. Their facility, which in the early stages was very impressive to us, made us envious. By the end of the first year,

56

however, their starting point was no longer such an advantage, and they became distributed more in accordance with their natural ability. There was not a single BIJ in the top class (of the twenty-some ranked classes into which we were divided), although there were some in the second class.

Many of them felt themselves on the horns of a dilemma: on the one hand, they harbored a natural affection for the Japan in which they had grown up; on the other hand, their country was at war with Japan. As one particularly agonized young man lamented to me, "I was born and raised in Japan, I grew up with Japanese friends. In fact I was so Japanized that when I first came back to the States for high school I felt like a stranger here. All I wanted was to go back to Japan. And now this war happens. We hear about all these atrocities. Are they the same people I grew up with? I am sure that some of them are in the Japanese army fighting against us. I wonder what I would do if I ran into one of them on some Pacific island." He, like many of the other BIJs, was hoping to find out by plunging deeply into matters Japanese—history, literature, and culture.

Apart from the BIJs were those who had lived in Japan for a time, even though they were not born there. One of them was the oldest of the enlisted men in the company, forty-two years of age, I believe, and he had been a businessman in Tokyo for many years. The Japanese he brought with him was uneducated, but it was rough and ready and it was serviceable. He knew it well enough, however, to realize that he needed a lot more polishing. We were then in the middle of the war, it must be recalled, and feelings had by now mounted to a fairly high point. Yet I remember him saying to me, "When you go to Japan—if we ever get there—one day, when you least expect it, you will fall madly in love. It may be in a bar, with some *mama-san* or hostess, or it might be in a geisha house, or it might be in someone's home. But sure as daylight, the lightning stroke will hit you." And despite the war, his image of the Japanese people he knew was a loving one.

I found this same nostalgic affection for the Japanese among

57

many in this group. One who had started his diplomatic career just before the war and had had to be repatriated on the last *Gripsholm* voyage, spoke of Japan with nothing but warmth. While waiting in Tokyo to return home after the war had broken out, he continued to associate with his personal friends, only being careful not to get them in trouble with the notorious *Kenpeitai,* or Military Police. In fact he recalled those days as among the most idyllic he had spent in Japan. No longer tied down by his office routine, he and a friend in the diplomatic service would travel to interesting places, go to the theater, quietly see their friends, study Japanese, and in general do all of the things they had always wanted to do but had not been able to because they had been so busy. It was his firm intention to return to Japan after the war and ultimately make his life there. He did.

The group that had studied Japanese in university was of a different type. One might ask why it is that people who have no personal familiarity with a country should want to learn its language. Was it that they had been turned on by Lafcadio Hearn and saw Japan as the romantic embodiment of their dreams of ancient Greece? So far as I recall, it was not. Richard Sneider, onetime deputy chief of mission of the American Embassy in Tokyo, who ended his diplomatic career as the U.S. ambassador to Korea, was not in my own class, but in the first Company A class formed at the University of Michigan. Sneider had started studying Japanese when he was a student at Brown University because he was majoring in international relations. "It was in 1942. I was majoring in international relations and I had to take some language. For some reason, Brown had just started an introductory course in Japanese and it seemed like a good deal, so I took it." From there he went into the army language school. His entire subsequent career has been tied up with Japan and the Far East.

The ASTP (Army Specialized Training Program) boys may very well have constituted a slight majority. They had all had close to a year of prior training in Japanese, and they knew how

58

to operate in that kind of setting. They came to Michigan in organized groups, sharing a common experience, and there was a strong tendency for them to form into cliques throughout the language school experience. They had come primarily from four schools, Yale University, the University of Michigan, the University of Chicago, and the University of Minnesota. Those from Michigan were naturally the most at home because they were on familiar ground, they had already established their local girlfriends, and they knew all the bars and joints. Their faction was therefore the most robust and high-swinging. They also knew the teachers, which gave them an additional advantage. Much of the interaction within the company followed along the ASTP clique lines, with the rest of us on the outside and obliged to form new links of interaction among ourselves.

The exceptions to these rules of selection included a small number of combat veterans of the Pacific theater who had received some special dispensation permitting them to go to the school, and the independents, who came through none of the specified channels. They were a colorful lot, indeed, ranging from a professional Russian translator who had laboriously taught himself to read over five thousand Chinese characters but who could scarcely pronounce them in an understandable fashion much less put together a Japanese sentence, to a fresh high school graduate from California who had been attracted to the study of Japanese because of the influence of his favorite teacher there.

Another was the redoubtable Sergeant Boris Yankoff, a White Russian, who turned out to be one of the real "characters" in the company. Yankoff was regular army. "I joined the army before I was eleven years old," he used to boast in his heavy Russian accent. His story was that he was always big for his age and that he joined the army at a time when sixteen was the minimum age but with a little fudging he was able to pass himself off as sixteen. Whether it was really true or not, one look at Yankoff was sufficient to convince one that he had indeed started his military career at eleven. Or even earlier.

"Maybe he was born in uniform," someone suggested.

Yankoff was rumored to have performed, during the Battle of Bougainville, one of those great senseless acts of heroism that defy rational explanation. One night, the story goes, he and several of his buddies crawled all the way over to the enemy camp, across the battlefield and through the barbed wire. What did they do when they got there? They copied down all of the signs in Japanese script they could see. Many of these, the story went, were actually nothing more significant than latrine signs. He did not know Japanese, but he copied the characters as faithfully as he could. Whether or not they contained much of combat intelligence value is not clear, but it was presumably as a reward for this extraordinary action—and perhaps his presumptive interest in Japanese script—that he was sent to our language school.

The Cast of Characters: Them

On the other side of the educational skirmish line there were the teachers, whom we always referred to by the Japanese term *sensei*, or maestro. In principle, they had all been selected on the assumption that they spoke the standard Tokyo dialect, and this was in fact the case. But many of them revealed just below the surface of their standard Japanese the ancestral traces, some even quite strongly, of their or their parents' provincial origin. Hiroshima and Kumamoto prefectures, the source of a large part of the Japanese immigration to the States, were the most common, but there was a scattering of residual accents from other places as well. All of this was helpful so that when we would run into some nonstandard accent in the field for the first time, we would not be thrown by the experience. Our predecessors, who went into combat intelligence teams throughout the Pacific and dealt with Japanese prisoners of war, must have had frequent occasion to be grateful to the *sensei* with nonstandard accents for giving them some advance preparation.

At the time I went to language school, there were a little over fifty teachers, all of them Japanese-Americans. In some of the other armed forces' language schools there were, I understand, a few non-Japanese—BIJs usually—teachers, but that was not the case in ours. The majority had had some college education, twenty-five in the United States and fifteen in Japan. Only twenty, however, had graduated from university at the time of their entry into the language school, two with M.A.'s and one with a doctorate. Some of them had come fresh from relocation camp, and after the first fearful looking around to see if the natives were friendly or not, they had by the time of my class already settled down with reasonable confidence that in a university community like Ann Arbor they would not be mistreated as "Japs" or fallen upon by local folk overfired with patriotism or just plain hoodlumism.

Nevertheless the deep wound had to be there—the suspicion of exclusion, the arm raised to ward off some insult, or rebuff, or hurtful action. All of them were, of course, thoroughly "cleared" before hiring, so presumably they were as pure as the driven snow, as loyal as any descendant of the *Mayflower* settlers. But even this did not suffice. In the officialese prose of an army report:

> Every officer and enlisted man detailed to the School was investigated to insure his loyalty to the United States. Many men and some officers were "blackballed" by some investigators simply because of racial prejudice or because the person being investigated had made a trip to Japan or had belonged to a Japanese athletic club. It is an established fact that numerous men and officers who were declared untrustworthy in the early days of the war later proved to be excellent soldiers and were decorated for service in combat.

Some of the professional military continued to nourish their suspicions about the Japanese-Americans, but in general this was not the case among the students. Nevertheless, there were some, particularly among our Southerners, who did not so easily overcome their prejudices. "They look all right on the surface," a Southern friend once said to me when he heard that I had been helping Japanese-Americans in the War Relocation Authority, "but you can never trust them. You never know what they are really thinking." But in general, even our small contingent of Pacific combat veterans, who were most likely to harbor dark feelings about the Japanese—after all, they had fought them, and one of our classmates had even been wounded—did not seem to do so. Everybody seemed to accept the student–teacher relation and was willing to accept the official judgment that they were loyal.

I wanted to be friendly. I was in the school and under their tender care only because I had become so involved with them in the War Relocation Authority. I was sympathetic to them and I understood, or at least had a feeling for, their problems. But the relation of teacher and student is always a delicate one. To act too friendly might suggest I was currying favor, calling for repayment of favors rendered. When I suspected, in one case upon trying to strike up a relationship outside the framework of the school, that this was so, I immediately ceased my efforts and never reopened them again.

It was only later, during the Occupation itself, that I was able to have a reasonably normal relationship with one of the *sensei*. He was younger than I, which made a difference, and our relationship had a good balance: I was his boss, but he could temper the raw reversal of our relationship by introducing me to all kinds of things that I did not know about Japan and that I might perhaps never have known, at least for a long time, without his expert guidance. It was through him that I had my first introduction to pottery and potters, to traditional weaving and dyeing in Kyoto, and to the pleasures of the Atami hot-spring spa. He was personally friendly with many potters, and on our frequent field trips around the country we made a point of arranging our schedule so that we were often in the neighborhood of interesting kilns and potters. For a while he had an affair with a geisha, something that at the time seemed to me very glamorous, and through him and his girl I learned —but only by word of mouth—about such arcane mysteries as the "nightingale crossing the valley," a pleasant game better left a mystery here.

But all of this was much later. During language school there was none of it. I could very well be wrong in my impression, but it seemed to me that, if anything, the Japanese-Americans avoided me. Their task, in the first few years after the start of the war and the evacuation, was to convince their doubting fellow Americans that they were loyal citizens and not subversive, racially destined agents of the enemy. I had somehow expected, since they knew that I was friendly, in fact, that I had worked for them, that they would make a point of particularly seeking me out. But this was not the case. It was as if knowing that I was already on their side, they no longer had any reason to blandish me or try to win me over. They seemed to take me for granted and therefore not make any particular efforts to be friendly.

I do not mean, however, that they were unfriendly. They were not. But it was as if my War Relocation Authority experience was not to enter into the equation of our relationship. We associated within the fixed frame of the student–teacher relationship, and if ever I chanced to make reference to the evacuation, their faces took on a puzzled, or even a pained, look, as if I had violated some tacit rule of the game, or as if I knew too much about them for them to feel comfortable with me.

All of this was somewhat puzzling. But soon I was quite willing to play the game by their rules and made no special efforts to be friendly. I accepted the student role in relation to the *sensei*. I also learned another important lesson—that people are not always grateful to those who help them. In fact, sometimes they resent them, perhaps because the sense of obligation to repay is irksome, perhaps because the helper has seen them in their moment of weakness and is not to be forgiven for having done so.

The teacher–student relationship has a built-in antagonism. Even though presumably both parties have a common objective—for the student to learn—it is an inherently hierarchical relation. The teacher is the superior, the student the inferior. The teacher has assets, or controls goods that the student lacks and desires. The teacher's evaluation affects the student's self-esteem and his future prospects. A student with bad grades would be dropped from the school and reassigned to ordinary military duty, losing this privileged assignment.

And even when the penalties were not that drastic, the teachers held a great deal of power over us. Every weekday evening, for example, we were required to spend two hours studying after dinner. But students with good grades during the preceding week, as I have already mentioned, were exempted from compulsory study and were free to study wherever they wished. Freedom to dispose of one's own movements is one of the most precious things in a military environment. Some of the men used their free time not to study but to visit girlfriends, go to the movies, and so on. But for the married men, whose wives or families had joined them in Ann Arbor, this evening freedom was even more precious. To lose it entrained not only the humiliation of having to study under supervision, it also meant that we would not be able to visit our wives and children except on weekends. So getting good grades was important, and it gave the teachers great power.

The ambiguities were compounded by the fact that the *sensei* were both Japanese *and* Americans. In general American society they were looked down upon, always having to prove themselves to their superiors. But in our small society, and only in relation to us, they were in the position of superiors, and it was we who had to prove ourselves to them and to win their favor. Undoubtedly they felt themselves in the same position in regard to their employers and superiors in the military hierarchy. But that made us, if one chose to look at it that way, the lowest of the low. And if one did choose to look at it that way, one might be resentful.

Fortunately, not many chose to do so, not the combat veterans nor even the Southerners, who sometimes unconsciously carried their primordial racial attitudes with them, despite their higher education. On the whole, the men of Company A were sympathetic to the Japanese-Americans and sympathetically inclined toward their problems.

If there is a kind of class antagonism between students and teachers, there is also a sense of common enterprise. Both are trying to achieve a common objective, and it is in the nature of the case that the mystery of learning has to be enacted in the student's mind. If their posture in relation to this enterprise is antagonistic, they are still on the same side.

The army, however, and the administrative cadres in charge of us, were on the other side, the enemy. Company A was not, after all, the usual army company. What its exact ranking was, I do not know, but its average IQ was certainly one of the highest in the army. This made us a company of intellectuals and students, that is, "eggheads," and we were a living outrage to the army cadres. They may have shared our objectives, in the sense that they were supposed to facilitate the process of our learning Japanese, but they did not share our experiences, nor did they understand or empathize with them. They also did not come from the same background—socially, educationally, intellectually, or in aspiration. This often made them resentful of us, and they would try to exercise the temporary ascendancy they had over us while we were still enlisted men and they were either officers or noncoms in charge of us. We had, therefore, to suffer a great deal of petty harassment and humiliation.

We were not, however, entirely without resources, although our weapons were mainly intellectual. One Saturday afternoon, for example, when we normally had our formal weekly inspection prior to being granted weekend leave, we had a visitation by an outside team of inspectors. Our company commander, in some anxiety about the outcome of this visitation, called the company together and made a special exhortation to us to do well and not disgrace him.

The inspectors came, but things did not go well. They found some dirty rifles and a few heads in need of haircuts. But above all they found dustballs under beds in some of the rooms. This became a *cause celèbre*, and our captain was desolated. He had always prided himself on being friendly to us, and he therefore felt that he had been betrayed by our bad inspection. We had let him down. On the following Monday or Tuesday, he called a meeting of the company to report to us the results of the inspection and to complain. His grammar was not equal to the occasion, and he delivered himself of a pronunciamento that remained forever engraved on our memories: "You guys have not shotten square with me."

Unfortunately for him, the phrase touched the fancy of the company and it was tossed back and forth around him like a basketball being thrown by professionals to tease some inept youngster. Our musicians also rose to the occasion and came up with a cruel lampoon. Using the tune of an old hymn, they sang:

> My eyes are dim,
> I cannot see,
> You have not shotten square with me,
> You have not shotten square with me.

The incident of the offending dustballs had another musical consequence:

> Balls, balls, balls
> Of dust were in the halls,
> Of dust were in the halls
> Of the third-floor Hinsdale Hall.

And this would lead into "My eyes are dim" once again.

III ☆
STUDYING JAPANESE

This, then, is the cast of characters of the fourth class in the Army Intensive Japanese Language School of Michigan. In Ann Arbor we were a company of about one hundred and sixty-five enlisted men and thirteen officer students. Fourteen months later, when we arrived at Fort Snelling, we were still in full force. But by August of 1945 the war came to an end and about half of the men elected to leave the army rather than complete the course and go on to further military service in the Occupation of Japan.

The Routine

In May 1944, however, our routine at Michigan was just starting. The program called for five hours of classwork and two hours of evening study five days a week. We had military training every day, usually at the nearby Burns Field, where we jogged, marched, and practiced close-order drill, all of which seemed totally irrelevant to us. Here we came under the control of our cadre and even of some of our classmates, whose experience or rank allowed them to act as instructors. If Boris Yankoff could not hack it in the language classes, here he was in his element. The military aspect of our training culminated in the Saturday morning inspection, often followed by parade drill. After Saturday morning inspection, we were free until Sunday night.

One or two afternoons a week we would have Japanese movies to improve our hearing of spoken Japanese. These were captured wartime movies brought back from the Pacific theater, and many of them were propaganda. The all-time hit in Company A was *China Night (Shina no Yoru)*, with Kazuo Hasegawa as the male lead and the popular actress Yoshiko Yamaguchi as the female lead. (She later played some minor roles in a few American movies under the name Shirley Yamaguchi.) At that time Yamaguchi was known as Rikōran, which is the Japanese pronunciation of the Chinese characters 李香蘭 , and was believed to be Chinese—somehow the idea became current among us that she was a Manchurian princess. We also heard rumors that she was really Japanese, although how that rumor started I do not know, since she only revealed her true identity after her repatriation to Japan in April 1946.

Perhaps it is a mark of the strange never-never world in which we lived—studying the enemy's language in the midst of a war with that very enemy—that we could entirely suspend our political views about Japan and look on the movie not as propaganda for the justice of Japan's cause in China but as pure spectacle. In any event, whatever the explanation, so far as I can recall, none of us looked upon the movie with hostility in spite of the fact that intellectually we, of course, knew that it was propaganda. But when Hasegawa's patient wooing of the bitter "Manchurian" Rikōran finally succeeded, and the two entered what to us was an "international," and what in the movie was a "Greater East Asian," relationship, we cheered as if he were one of us, instead of one of the enemy. To some extent, this curious reaction may be attributable to the quality of the acting, but I doubt that that was the entire explanation. For many of us it was a foretaste of what we ourselves would one day experience in what we were sure would be an occupied Japan—the local maidens' bitterness against the conquerors finally melting away before the irresistible pressure of men good and true. Rikōran became the sweetheart of Company A. It was every man's ambition to know her, and many vowed that the first thing they would do on reaching Japan was search her out, and . . . and . . . and . . . Whether they did or not, I never did find out.

Every morning of the week, except Sunday, the men of Company A were awakened at 6 A.M., not by bugles, because this might disturb the university neighborhood in which we were located, but by floor monitors. Within fifteen minutes we were supposed to fall out into the street for roll call, already dressed, showered, and shaved. Roll call was followed by breakfast at 7 A.M. By 7:45 beds were made, preparations completed, and we marched off to our first class. Classes continued until 12:00, and then we marched back for lunch in the dining room of the dormitory.

There were always long lines awaiting their turn at the dining room, and to the outside visitor it must have been startling to see us lined up, studying our "*kanji* cards"—two- by three-inch cardboard cards with a Chinese character and its principal compounds on one side and pronunciation and the English translation on the other—first staring at the card and muttering the pronunciations *sotto voce* to ourselves and then turning the cards over to see if we had guessed correctly, or as often happened, writing the characters in the air and then pausing for a moment to think and then erase a mistake in the air. At Michigan the cadre members were accustomed to this and after a while paid no attention. But later, at Fort McClelland, it drove the training cadre wild. It only confirmed the already entrenched conviction that college students were all crazy. Lunch was followed by the afternoon classes, which finished at 3 P.M.

The academic program was followed by military drill, and then at 5 P.M., we marched back to the barracks, showered, napped, wrote letters, or studied until dinner time. After dinner, we went off to study, mostly under the eyes of the *sensei*

69

in the library, the privileged others off to their separate pads—the married men to their homes in order to be with their families, the single men to their rooms or whatever other convenient spots they could find for study or for amusement.

After study was finished, there followed a period of free time, and by 11 P.M. it was lights out. There was often a bed check to be sure everybody was properly back in. This used to be a further irritation to those of us who already resented the infantilizing treatment to which we were subjected as enlisted men.

The entire student body was divided into ranked classes (which we called *kumi*, using the Japanese word) on the basis of degree of achievement, into between twenty and twenty-five classes of seven to eight students each. The highest was Class One and the lowest whatever the bottom number happened to be at that particular time. Every week or two, we were reassigned on the basis of the previous week's performance in class and test. I myself started in the bottom class, then Class Twenty-two, I believe, because I was the only one in the company who had no previous background in Japanese. But during the year I moved up steadily, eventually ending in the first class. Therefore, I had occasion to experience every class level and to have studied, even though for a short time, with almost every student in one class or another. Although there were thirteen officer students among us—seven second lieutenants, four first lieutenants, and two captains—it was striking that not one was in any of the higher classes. The top classes consisted entirely of enlisted men.

The lack of relation between rank and performance posed a problem: if we did so much better than these officer students, why were they officers and we enlisted men? Eventually, of course, this anomalous situation would straighten itself out and legitimacy be restored because we were all one day to be commissioned as officers. But the Nisei had the right to raise the same question with even more justice. They were better at the assigned task than we were, but we would end up as commissioned officers and they would not. "Caucasian officers usually

70

headed up each unit," writes Joseph Harrington in his history of the Nisei participation in the Pacific War (*Yankee Samurai*), "an item that did not go down so well with Nisei . . . Nisei could not see why men who knew less Japanese than themselves, and often had no more education than some NCOs on the team, got commissions and they didn't." Toward the end of the war this began to change, but for a long time this was the structure of the situation, and the changes came grudgingly.

We became painfully aware of it when, at Fort Snelling, we first came into contact with Nisei and experienced their resentment directly. The tension, which manifested itself in dozens of petty incidents, reached its climax when two of our men were badly beaten by Hawaiian Nisei. One was hospitalized with an eye injury that was feared might be permanent (fortunately it was not). The other was stabbed by some stilettolike weapon that penetrated so deeply that a few millimeters in one direction would have reached his lungs and a few millimeters in the other direction his aorta.*

At eight every morning we were in class in Angell Hall. This building became so much a part of our lives that we had our own little in-joke about it, a Chinese character to express this daily occurrence, "to go to Angell Hall" (衏). This is made up of the Chinese characters for "angel" (天人) surrounded by the two elements of the character for "to go" (行). The Japanese call their own homemade characters, that is, those they made up in Japan rather than took from China, *wasei*, or "made" (*sei*) in "Japan" (*wa*). This was our first *beisei*, that is, "made" (*sei*) in "America" (*bei*). Every hour during the academic day we had a different instructor and subject, thus being exposed not only to a wide range of content but also to a wide range of speaking

---

*One of the Nisei participants in those events, then a graduate student in sociology and today professor of sociology at the University of California in Santa Barbara, has written a full account of them: see Tamotsu Shibutani, *The Derelicts of Company K—A Sociological Study of Demoralization*, Berkeley: University of California Press, 1978.

71

styles and pronunciations. Our daily subjects invariably included conversation, reading, dictation, and translation. Saturday morning was the time we usually had our most serious spit-and-polish army-type inspections—rooms, beds, clothing, rifles. If one did badly in the Saturday inspection, one might lose all or part of one's weekend leave privileges. If all went well, we were free for the weekend.

The Study of Japan: Area Study

Area study, that is, Japanese history, geography, politics, economics, and literature, was not part of our curriculum. This was, both at the time and in retrospect, surprising in view of our ultimate mission, but there seemed to be an assumption that the amount of time available in our program did not allow for any diversion from intensive language study. At the lower-level Army Specialized Training Program, area studies had figured prominently, but the consensus was that this had come at the expense of language intensiveness. The odd result was that we carried on our study of the Japanese language without reference to the society and culture within which that language was spoken. Of course, many of the men in the company had some personal experience that provided a context: the BIJs, for example, or those who had lived in Japan or studied Japanese subjects in university, or even the ASTP graduates. But I was not among them. I literally knew nothing, except possibly what little still clung to me from John Embree's *Suye Mura*.

The expectation apparently was that the students would acquire their knowledge of Japan on their own, either through reading or indirectly through the materials that were used in studying the language. The more advanced Naganuma readers, for example, contained a great deal about Japanese society, politics, and economics, and there were also readings at various levels from Japanese literature.

In any event, to some extent, the original expectation seems to have been met. Many of us did a lot of reading on Japan, picking up books from the library either suggested by the *sensei*, who were not, of course, necessarily familiar with English-language materials, or by the more knowledgeable men in our company. The movies also were helpful. Despite their usually propagandistic character, one was able to sense from them styles of living, rhythms of daily life, and ways of thinking about life, personal relations, and the war. The fact, for example, that we never saw any kissing in these films was very striking, and it suggested that Japanese morality was very different from American, at least at that point in time. The sight of Rikōran brimming with love, indeed melting in love, revealing her feelings only in slight movements of the eyes, a gentle inclination of the neck, a fleeting smile, was infinitely seductive. But it was very different from the way the American women we knew would act in the same situation and gave us a different image of what women could be.

The main thing I read was Sir George Sansom's classic *A Short Cultural History of Japan*. The book was to me an exciting revelation, but it does not deal with modern Japan at all; it ends in 1867. And so, despite my reading, Japan still remained a remote land, a separate entity off somewhere in time and space, and did not necessarily have any connection with the present day. My task eventually would be to bring the two pieces together, the pre-Meiji world before 1868, already fixed in its timeless history, and the modern world. But that task still lay ahead of me. I did not have an image of modern Japan that I could even begin to try to bring into adjustment with the historical image that I was acquiring.

I also came across an old, battered copy of an obscure work, *Early Institutional Life of Japan*, by an obscure scholar at that time scarcely known in either the United States or in Japan—Kan'ichi Asakawa. Asakawa had gone to Yale University after finishing his work at Waseda (then still a "college" by Japanese legal definition, not the university it is today) and took his Ph.D. in 1903 or thereabouts. He remained until the early postwar days carrying on his scholarly work at Yale virtually without an audience. His doctoral dissertation was on the Taika

Reform of A.D. 645, and I learned much from it. But this was also about ancient Japan, and it no more prepared one for understanding post-Meiji, much less wartime Japan, than a study of Homer's *Iliad* would prepare one for understanding modern Greece.

But since I found Asakawa so fascinating, I followed up on some of his all too little-known studies of Japanese feudalism. Asakawa was a distinguished feudalist and he was rather well known in this select field, particularly in Europe. Almost all of his serious scholarly writing was in English. Since I was an anthropologist, I had a natural bias toward comparative studies, and his comparative analyses of Japanese and Western feudalism came to me as a revelation. It was only with the much later work of John W. Hall of Yale University that I found anything that went beyond the point Asakawa had already reached before World War I. When Hall went to Yale from Michigan (he was, incidentally, a navy, not an army, language school graduate), he dusted off many of Asakawa's manuscripts and brought about a modest Asakawa revival.

In one of the footnotes to an obscure article of his, "Village Government in 1600," I came across a reference to a remote village in the upper reaches of the Iyo River in Shikoku that caught my fancy:

> The Iya-yama villages (in the province of Iyo) ... were completely protected from the outside world by high mountains and deep ravines. In the fourteenth century, this place was occupied by a few hardy warriors with their retainers, who resisted encroachments, and stood against a powerful baron when all the rest of Shikoku had succumbed to him. ...
>
> Throughout the Tokugawa period, [the] privileges of the chiefs remained undisturbed. ... At the fall of the feudal government in 1869, Iya-yama was found to contain nearly 10,000 souls ... the chiefs were warriors, and owed a knight's service; they held their post by heredity; and they held their tenants as serfs. ...

74

It would be interesting to visit this region today and study its present conditions. A citizen of Iyo who has recently travelled across Iya-yama observes that it is still largely inaccessible, that the families of the chiefs were still greatly respected by the peasants, and that many of the latter were still intractable and defiant.

I, too, thought "it would be interesting to visit this region." So, in 1947, when I was on a trip to Kōchi Prefecture in connection with the Occupation's fishery reforms, I made a side trip to Iyo and completed one of my life's objectives when I found the village of his footnotes. It was still an isolated village, with descendants of rustic samurai residents on their lands and exercising a strong traditional form of control. The first sight that greeted me was of men walking huge logs, weighing up to one hundred kilograms, down the narrow twisting trails. The logs were cradled in a forked carrying device over their heads, the whole held in place by a specially fitted harness. When there was a sharp turn in the trail, they had to turn their heads and bodies slowly so as not to build up momentum that would swing them over the edge. When they got tired, they would place a kind of cane with a flat top under the waist portion of the cradle harness to take the weight off their backs and shoulders. Strong young backs performed this labor, but even for them the strain was sometimes so great that you could see them trembling in their sweat like aspen leaves until they could find a spot to rest their burdens. Many years later in the Himalayas, near Dalhousie, I saw a similar technique being used by Nepali loggers. They were smaller men and less sturdy than the men of Iyo, but they carried heavier logs and, instead of centering the weight overhead, they carried the logs tied to their backs.

In Iyo, I also learned for the first time about the agreeable traditional practice of *yobai*, or "night crawling." This had been quite common in many rural areas of old Japan, a form of sanctioned premarital sex or, in some cases, a kind of trial marriage. An adolescent girl would be given a room in some relatively isolated part of the house and there during the night she could receive lovers if she wished. A young suitor would literally save face by covering his face in strips of cloth so that if he were rejected neither side need acknowledge his identity. But once the girl became pregnant, it was expected that the responsible young man would marry her. Young men, before their marriage, would live in a special dormitory, a kind of "age grading" similar to what anthropologists report from Polynesia, and it was from these dormitories that they would take off on their night-crawling business. When some of the old men, sitting around and drinking beer, said something about *yobai*, my anthropological ears perked up and I started interviewing them about whether Iyo still had the youth dormitory and whether *yobai* still played a role in mate selection. They all laughed. "Young people today are very peculiar," one explained to me. "They don't go in for that kind of thing any more. They think it's old-fashioned and barbarian. I can't understand why they are so puritanical about things. It was a great system." The other old men agreed vigorously.

In the language school, however, none of my readings made Japan come alive to me as a living society. Of contemporary Japan I knew little more than what I read in the media or heard from my buddies who knew something about it. Perhaps if Ruth Benedict's *The Chrysanthemum and the Sword*, which was to remain, until recently, the most influential postwar book on Japan, had come out by then, I would have been more attentive than I was. During one of my furloughs from language school, which I spent in New York, I had dinner one night with Margaret Mead and her husband, Gregory Bateson, and they told me about Benedict's work. But on that occasion there were other subjects that were more interesting to us—including their New Guinean and Indonesian experiments with the use of motion pictures in ethnography. Besides, no publications from the wartime project on Japan that Benedict, Geoffrey Gorer, the English anthropologist, and Weston LaBarre, the psychiatrist, were engaged in had yet reached the academic journals that I might have chanced to come across. Benedict's book was published only in 1946, when I was already in Japan. So it was not part of my intellectual preparation for Japan.

The Classroom

On our very first day of class we were instructed in the basic rule of the program: no English was to be used in the classroom. If we wanted to ask a question, say about the meaning of a word or phrase or about a grammatical point, we had to do it in Japanese, and the instructor was to answer us in Japanese. So far as I recall, this practice was followed in all of the classes I was in.

For the first several weeks, we were given conversation lessons, at least in the lower classes where I had been placed. Every day we received mimeographed materials, freshly prepared by the instructors, providing drill in conversation, vocabulary, sentence and grammatical patterns, and brief explanations, or, more often, alternative ways to get at the same idea. We recited either by reading from these forms or, in the course of time, by memorizing them and then acquiring the ability to apply the patterns to other related situations. The teaching technique required that traditional types of grammatical explanations not be given, so the teachers developed great skill in explaining by developing a point in Japanese, by providing us with indirect clues, by stimulating us to discover for ourselves the underlying principle involved in a complicated construction and, if worse came to worst, by direct pointing.

In the upper classes, where the students were already well advanced in their Japanese studies, the simple phonetic scripts, the *hiragana* and the *katakana* (which were syllabaries rather than alphabets), were taught immediately. But we in the lower classes were judged too far behind to start with writing. So our first weeks were spent in conversation classes. Only after about three weeks or so were we started on the syllabic writing, and then two weeks later we began our work on Chinese ideographs, the *kanji*.

A few of the students already had a considerable repertoire of Chinese characters as a result of their own studies. But most of us started from the beginning. The teaching materials in American universities at the time the war broke out had been designed for an entirely different approach to the teaching of Japanese. In most cases the university programs had concentrated primarily on reading, with a heavy dose of grammar, and very little, if any, conversation. For this purpose, existing texts served well. But the army's intensive program represented an entirely new approach, and the existing materials were totally inadequate.

The result was that throughout the program, in both the army and the navy, heavy reliance was placed on the Naganuma course brought back by the prewar language officers and adapted by the instructors throughout the course of the program. Teachers were constantly preparing fresh mimeographed materials as in our first few weeks, and sometimes we had the impression that the materials had only been prepared the very night before, and most likely in a late session.

The Naganuma readers were a series of graded texts, starting from a very elementary level and moving up, volume by volume, to a very advanced adult level. The early volumes utilized a great deal of material from elementary school textbooks, the middle ones used materials appropriate to middle school level, and the later volumes were at the high school and university level, with a great deal of literature, newspaper material, magazine articles, and so on.

In addition to the specially prepared materials and the readers, we also used Professor Yamagiwa's then new text entitled *Modern Conversational Japanese*. Although this volume was specifically designed to help in conversational Japanese and, therefore, presumably represented a departure from the traditional American academic emphasis on grammar, there was constant complaint that it was still too old-fashioned, a throwback to the old reading and grammar types of textbook. One of the complaints was that we were required to memorize the highly abstract and idiosyncratic technical grammatical terms invented by Professor Yamagiwa, such as "conclusive-attributive," "concessive," "imperfective," and so on. A good deal of gentle spoofing took place about this grammatical jargon, and some of the men invented plausible sounding nonsense terms of their own—such as the "passive contraceptive," the "imperfect contraceptive," and the "conjunctive inversion"—and teased some of the teachers with them. One of the company wits wrote a learned essay on *bungotai*, or "literary style," which started out as follows: "*Bungo* is the written or 'mysterious East' form of the Japanese language. . . . When the predecessors of the present Yamato race, inspired by the slogan, 'On to Tokyo,' crossed the Chōsen strait and began their slow occupation of the volcanic Japanese mainland, they spoke only in conclusive-attributives."

The Rose-Innes bilingual character dictionary was our staple, but we were also required to learn how to use an all-Japanese dictionary as well. The tens of thousands of Chinese characters are classified on the basis of an identifying element in each of them called the radical. There are two hundred and fourteen of them. One of the important ways we learned to master the Chinese characters, and also to use the dictionary, was by memorizing as many of these radical elements as we could. These were so deeply ingrained into us that still today, more than thirty-five years later, the numbers of the radicals leap to mind instantly when I have to look up a character: "man," radical 9; "tree," radical 75; "flower," radical 140; etc. I do not recall exactly how many *kanji* it was planned for us to learn, but I do recall that some of the men set themselves their own objectives. Several decided to memorize the entire Rose-Innes, which consisted of five thousand characters. The school aimed only to provide us with a base from which we could go ahead on our own and, therefore, it emphasized exposure to a large number of *kanji*, even if we could not absorb all of them, and training in the use of the basic tools, such as dictionaries.

As we advanced in our understanding of the language, new

materials were prepared for us—military vocabulary, newspaper styles, literary style, formal epistolary style—and we were always receiving new glossaries, word lists, specialized vocabularies, and reading materials. While, in many cases, the intention was only to familiarize us with these materials, not to make us expert, there were always some members of the class who went very far indeed with them. The *"kanji* king" (today, Professor Leon Hurvitz of the University of British Columbia), I recall, was already writing letters in *sōrōbun*, the formal epistolary style, while he was still at Michigan. But then, by that time, he also knew at least ten thousand characters.

It was his claim, supported by general consensus, to know the number of every *kanji* in the *Ueda daijiten*, the large Japanese dictionary that we used. Whether he actually knew every single one, I am not prepared to say, but I did have an experience with him that was awesome. I had received a New Year's card from a Chinese friend with one character in it that I could not read. I looked it up in my Rose-Innes dictionary but could not find it. So I called on Leon and asked him if he knew it. At the barest glance he said, "Yes. That character is not in the Rose-Innes, nor is it in the *Ueda daijiten*. You will find it in *Fuzanbō*, number such-and-such." The implication of this flat statement was breathtaking. To say it was not in the *Ueda* he had to know all fourteen thousand characters in that dictionary. To say it was number such-and-such in the *Fuzanbō* implied equally that he knew all the characters in that dictionary and, moreover, knew them so well that he could locate them by number. That evening I looked up the two dictionaries in our study hall. Sure enough the *kanji* was not in the *Ueda daijiten*, and it was in the *Fuzanbō*, just where he said it was.

IV ✩

THE LEARNING OF LANGUAGES

Getting into Japanese

The learning of a foreign language is a complex process that involves not simply the ingestion of a new body of information but rather a vast transformation of the self. The self, in effect, is reprogrammed, and this process is not only psychological but, it seems to me, physiological as well. I speak several languages, and I find that my personality, my movements, my gestures, and my frame of mind seem to change when I shift from one language to another. When I speak French, I feel—probably falsely—lucid, polemic, plausible, persuasive, unexpected, paradoxical. French is a preferred language for seduction. But when I move into Spanish, I become a different person. In order to get the cadences and intonation right, I find myself automatically making gestures like the Mexicans do. It seems to me that I am more *macho*, more forceful and dogmatic, sometimes poetic, and often earthy. When I speak Japanese, I am always surprised at how polite a person I can be, something that I do not particularly think about myself when I speak English.

With each language I speak, it seems to me that I become a

81

different person. I respond to people differently, and I often see things somewhat differently. When I watch professional interpreters faithfully transmitting nuances from one language to another, I am filled with admiration. When I go from one language to another, it is myself that changes.

The learning of foreign languages, it seems to me, involves some kind of physiological change. The mouth, lips, and facial muscles must learn to articulate new sounds in new cadences and intonations; the ear must learn to distinguish the new phonemes from out of the flux of sound; and the mind must learn automatically, which means unconsciously rather than consciously, to think in the categories of thought, the grammatical structure, and the word order of the other language. All of this requires time, and the more distant the new language is from one's starting point, the longer the time required to make the physiological change.

How much these differences are a function of the language environment in which one is raised, rather than of race, came home very forcibly to me through an early experience of mine in Japan. I was walking down the street in Tokyo one day looking at a young man scurrying ahead of me. It occurred to me with absolute certainty that this young man was an American Nisei and not a Japanese. Why, I could not then say. Both Nisei and Japanese obviously have the same racial features. Nevertheless, they are easily distinguished by the subtle, and even not so subtle, clues provided by facial movements, the set of the lips, and the interplay of eye and lips that are distinctive to each language. Those raised speaking English look different from their racial brothers raised speaking Japanese. The Nisei who was responsible for bringing the revelation home to me that day was, I later realized, walking with a long stride, lifting his shoes clear of the pavement; most Japanese, at least at that time, would tend toward a more shuffling pace, as if they were wearing traditional Japanese straw sandals, *zōri*, or wooden clogs, *geta*, rather than shoes.

In the first stage of learning a foreign language one starts out with a small stock of words and a few basic sentence patterns. At first the stock of vocables and grammatical forms is limited. My own Japanese vocabulary was small and I could speak only in the present indicative (that "conclusive-attributive" again!) except for fixed, or petrified phrases. During the first phase, I consolidated this range and managed to handle it fairly well. But I began to realize, particularly as I spoke with people, that there were many things missing—other tenses, modes, vocabulary, etc. When I became aware of them, I would look for some appropriate grammatical exposition in our texts, or more likely I would either ask directly (when I could formulate the question properly), or I would start sentences that required a correct form or a correct word for completion and then wait for my protagonist to supply it to me. It was a kind of sentence-completion technique, with the environment itself filling out the unfinished portion of the sentence. As I reached the stage in my language development where I keenly felt the need for these forms and words, I seized them the moment they made their appearance and held them firmly. Then I would move on to another phase of consolidation.

But whenever I first started from one consolidated ground to the next higher level, there would be a period of wobbling about, in which I could neither control my earlier ground as well as before nor stabilize my control of the new level. It was discouraging to feel that you had lost ground you thought you already commanded. But gradually I began to lose my sense of panic about this phenomenon. I realized that it was essential for moving on to the next stage.

My greatest feeling of triumph came one day when I suddenly understood how to use one of the Japanese nominalizing forms—which happen to be difficult for English speakers—for example, *tanomareta kara soko ni itta* wake *desu* ("the *reason* I went there is that I was asked"). For a long time I had been feeling that the simple past tense I used was not adequate to express what I wanted to say, and then all of a sudden the phrase leaped out of a sentence to which I was listening as

83

clearly as if it had an aura. From then on I began to use these nominalizing forms as if they were the most natural thing to do.

And yet to a speaker of English, or of any of the other European languages, they are not. Learning a European language takes less time for us than learning Japanese because a good part of the process is translation rather than complete transformation. Grammatical categories, basic word order, underlying concepts are all sufficiently similar among the Western European languages that they are fairly easily mastered. But in the case of Japanese, the forms are radically different. The word order is almost directly reversed, with postpositions instead of prepositions—for example, one says "the house *to*" rather than "to the house"; the verbs are at the end rather than at earlier points in the sentence; the negative is expressed as a conjugation of the verb rather than by specific "not" words; the tenses are not exactly the same as in the European languages; underlying concepts organizing the phenomenal world are often different; there are no relative pronouns; and many words have radically different ranges of meaning.

Therefore, while three or four months of intensive study of a European language will yield the English speaker three or four months of speaking ability, this is not the case with Japanese. For us, learning Japanese is a threshold phenomenon: below a certain point very little seems to happen; it is only after there has been a sufficient accumulation that one is able to start using the language the way someone studying a European language is able to do from Day One. What this means, of course, is that in the learning of Japanese, there must always be a long period of intensive study during which the psychological and physiological transformations I have referred to take place. Once they are completed, the learner can move ahead at a pace more similar to what he would have been able to do with a European language a year earlier. While there is obviously some individual variation in this process, a good rule of thumb is that one full year is required. Anything less does not yield proportionate results.

Let me emphasize again that these considerations apply only to speakers of Western European languages. Speakers of other languages, such as Korean, Mongolian, Turkish, Uzbek, Hungarian, and so on, that is, what the philologists call the Ural-Altaic, or even its Finno-Ugric subgroup, may very well find Japanese easier in the early stages because they share important grammatical techniques, concepts, and devices, and sometimes even basic sentence structure and word order. I remember a Mongolian scholar who came as a visiting professor to the University of Washington when I was on the faculty there, telling me that "Japanese is an easy language; just like Mongolian." After all the hard work it had taken me to learn Japanese, I was disgusted.

So we were fortunate that in the very midst of a war, when our age-mates were in combat all over the world, we were granted this rare opportunity to spend that necessary one year of full-time intensive concentration that is required to carry us over the threshold. As we all had different starting points in the language, everybody reached the critical threshold at a different point in time. For me it took the entire year, a year marked by a series of significant discoveries and stages.

In our very first conversation lesson, we had a sequence that went something as follows (in Japanese):

Please bring me that book (*Sono hon o motte kite kudasai*).
Yes, I will (*Kashikomarimashita*).

The phrase that I have translated as "Yes, I will" is, in Japanese, the single world *kashikomarimashita*. This was at first almost my undoing; eventually it turned out to be my first major revelation. To start with, it was long. As pronounced in Japanese, it had eight syllables—*ka-shi-ko-ma-ri-ma-shi-ta*—and since at first they were to me nonsense syllables, I had difficulty putting them all together in the right order. I went around practicing it for days.

In the second place, although in English we would expect it to be in the present tense, it was in fact in the past tense. (The present tense would be *kashikomarimasu*; the phrase we had just learned was the past form, *kashikomarimashita*.) Obviously, then, the so-called past form in Japanese is not (or at least not always) the same kind of time indicator that it is in English; it also seemed to have the function of making the term more respectful. But that suggested that degrees of respect were incorporated in what we in English would regard as a simple matter of tense. This insight was soon reinforced when I learned that although the standard term for "thank you" (*arigatō gozaimasu*) was in the present tense, the sense of gratitude could be deepened by using it in the past tense (*arigatō gozaimashita*).

But there was still more to be learned from that one single term: how important relative status position, or hierarchical ranking, was in speaking Japanese. *Kashikomarimashita* is an extremely polite, or more accurately, a self-humbling term that places the speaker a great distance below the person he is addressing. It is the kind of answer we can imagine a humble servitor giving a great king, or a lowly slave addressing to an exalted master, whose sense might perhaps be roughly rendered into English as "I tremble in awe before you." Such language might have been used in feudal England, but other than as a phrase found in older literature, or as a joke, it was not part of the contemporary repertoire of English. This meant either that traditional feudal class concepts still lived in Japan or that such terms had become petrified as fixed conventions of conversation.

How sensitive such matters could be I realized when one of the BIJs told several of us beginners very seriously: "Don't answer them with '*kashikomarimashita*.' That's a trick to make you act humble with them. *Kashikomarimashita* is used only by servants to their masters. They're trying to tell you that we Americans should be the servants of the Japanese." Since he was a BIJ, a status that in the early period carried some authority with us, this was worrisome. But when one saw the serious pedagogical concern on the faces of the teachers, it was hard to believe that we were the victims of a subtle plot to undermine the morale of American soldiers by making them think they were inferior to the Japanese. When I asked my friend what we should say instead of *kashikomarimashita* in that context, he suggested a few terms at a lesser degree of politeness (*yoshi* or *yoroshii*), at all events something a little brusque to show those teachers who had the power in this man's country. Since I had no independent basis for making a judgment myself I asked one of the men who had lived in Japan for a long time. "Nonsense," he laughed. "*Kashikomarimashita* is certainly humble, but humble forms in Japan are a sign of respect to elders, teachers, employers, or other superiors. So you are not lowering yourself when you use them."

Thus it is that one single term, within the particular context presented in our very first lesson—not to mention my slightly paranoiac BIJ friend's angry reaction to it—raised the very profoundest of questions about Japanese, about English, and about Japanese society and its historical development in comparison with Western historical development.

It seems to me that every new form and almost every new word raised similar far-reaching questions. Learning Japanese was like learning a new set of categories for describing the universe. Or perhaps a better comparison is with literature. Reading novels, poetry, and even scholarly works opens the reader to new ranges of experience that he has not personally had. One can experience vicariously, and the vicarious experience can bring about changes as profound as if we had actually had the experiences ourselves. Since we humans are finite beings, and we can only experience so much within a single moment or within the span of our lifetime, literature enables us to transcend the limitations of time and space and to have experiences that occur outside the reach of our physiological perceptors.

A new language does something similar. It brings one new experiences, new ways of perceiving reality, new emotions, new aesthetic insights, new understandings, new ways of perceiving oneself. These insights first came to us at the very lowest levels of the language—greetings, thanking, and so on. Take, for example, the Japanese "How are you?" (*Ogenki desu ka*; literally, "Are you well?"), or "Has there been any change?" (*Okawari wa gozaimasen ka*) and its response, "Thanks to you" (*Okagesama de*; literally, "Under your shadow") by contrast with the English "How are you?" "I am well, thank you." At first glance, they seem reasonably close to each other. But the Japanese phrase says "thanks *to* you . . . " whereas English only says "thank you," which means something different—not "on account of you," or "because of you," but rather "thank you for being interested." An old-fashioned European might say "thanks to God," or "thank God," just as Muslims say "thanks to Allah." But the implication of the Japanese is entirely different: that I am obligated to you for the state of my health, that somehow you have something to do with my present condition of good health. The English has no such implication.

It was only some years later that I acquired a technical vocabulary to describe the relation implied by this behavior. It falls into a form of interpersonal interaction that the Japanese psychiatrist Takeo Doi characterizes as *amae*. The word *amae* comes from the Japanese word for "sweet," and in its verb form, *amaeru*, it means "to behave in such a way as to elicit favor or loving behavior from the other party"; the self is abased, the other party exalted, and the self placed at the other party's tender mercies. The word for "indulging" someone, or "spoiling" someone (*amayakasu*) comes from the same root of "sweet," thus meaning in effect to "treat someone sweetly." So the simple response, "Thanks to you," to the question, "How are you," revealed what Dr. Doi describes as the need to *amaeru*, or seek favor, and the importance of interpersonal obligation in Japan by contrast with the relative coolness reflected in the standard English usage.

The common word for thank you, *arigatō* (more politely, *arigatō gozaimasu*; and even politer still, *arigatō gozaimashita*), provided another example. Its literal meaning is not "thanks" or something to do with gratitude; it is "it is hard." This derivation was extremely instructive; it pointed to the feeling that reciprocal obligation, favor and its repayment, are relations that are burdensome in Japan, and thus "hard." Implied in that simple word was an entire theory of interpersonal obligation. Western academic sociology has only recently discovered something like it in the still fashionable "exchange theory." But for Americans, to whom the term "thank you" implies a far lesser degree of gratitude, or more accurately, obligation, the term was very revealing.

Studying Japanese also sensitized us to alternative ways of perceiving the world of phenomena. The exact relation between words and their referents in the real world is a very complex one, part of the very technical fields of philosophy, semantics, and semiotics. In any event, even words that presume to refer to specific concrete objects can never fully specify them. The word "glass," for example, instantly brings to our minds a particular kind of drinking utensil. But the reality of such an object may be described not only by the material of which it is made but by its shape, color, function, size, relative height and width, and so on. "Glass" is therefore only a conventionally agreed upon code word that most people will instantly associate with the type of drinking utensil I have referred to.

But any reality might just as easily be referred to by some other attribute than the one that happens to have been conventionally settled upon. I had a minor epiphany one day when I looked up the word "pot" in the dictionary. In Japanese, the words to render it meant literally a "water container," or "an object into which water is poured" (*mizuire, mizusashi*). In English, the corresponding objects—pot, or jug—are described not by their function but by their shape. (According to the *Oxford English Dictionary*, a pot is "a vessel of cylindrical or other rounded form and rather deep than broad, commonly made of earthenware or metal"; a jug is "a deep vessel . . . usually with a cylindrical or swelling body or one that tapers upward . . .") Neither the Japanese nor the English word, of course, describes the object; but the one uses the function as a code and the other uses the shape as the code. Later on I would make the ironic discovery that Japanese had absorbed both of the English words whole, "pot" becoming *potto* and "jug" becoming *jakki* ("jug" first pronounced Japanese-style as *jaggi* and then because of the hard double *g* becoming *jakki*).

So we quickly began to learn that Japanese and English could refer to the same reality from different angles of view, not necessarily emphasizing the same aspect. A striking example is the road sign one frequently sees on the highway—BUMP, or BUMP AHEAD. On Japanese roads this situation would be described by the word *dansa,* or "difference in level." The Japanese term describes the physical characteristic of the difference in level; the English word refers to the experience you will have if you drive over it. Or the fact that in Japanese the generic term for wheeled vehicles is "wheel" (*kuruma*), which refers to the distinctive fact of having wheels, whereas in English the generic term for exactly the same entity is "vehicle," which refers to its function of carrying people or things. (We also sometimes use the word "wheels" in the same sense, "Do you have wheels?" The use, however, is not standard.)

The study of Japanese also began to make it clear to me—and I am sure to most of my buddies—that the phenomenal world is a continuum and that it can be divided linguistically in many different ways. One of the central aesthetic categories in Japanese, for example, is the word *shibui.* By now it is widely recognized, and not only among those familiar with Japanese art. Many people have recorded their difficulties translating it into English. The question arises, therefore, as to whether the experience is unique to the Japanese so that the term cannot be translated in any other language. I would argue that is not the case. The Japanese term is a code for a delimited range of reality having particular characteristics. English speakers do not define that range of experiences by a single term. Not that they are not aware of such qualities, but they must describe them by a different set of code words that relate back metaphorically to different realities and experiences. The Japanese term suggests an elegance coming from astringency, spareness, the understated, unobtrusive beauty, the low key; in English, these qualities can be described, but not by a single term that conveys a single total perception. Edward Seidensticker, the distinguished authority on Japanese literature and translator of the tenth-century classic *The Tale of Genji*, has suggested "austere." I would agree that anything *shibui* is austere; but it seems to me that it is also more than that.

The same is true of all the other organized categories of perception—aesthetic, poetic, social. Two of the other principal aesthetic concepts in Japanese, known as *wabi* and *sabi*, also opened our eyes to different experiences, or to a different way of looking at experiences that we were already familiar with. *Wabi* means subdued, quiet, but it carries the echo of its original meaning of wretched, lonesome, comfortless, grieving. *Sabi* refers to the quality of elegant simplicity, but of the special kind that must be related to its original meaning of rust and patina. While we do not have specific terms in English for these concepts, we are perfectly capable of expressing them in other words.

Social concepts raised similar issues. From any given position in a structure—whether school, company, club, or military unit—there are three positions: predecessors; fellows of one's own cohort; and followers. For us, these concepts are essentially temporal, or sequential. In Japanese, the terms used for these sequences additionally imply a set of differential relations and obligations. To a predecessor, or senior (*senpai*), one owes deference, respectfulness, and obedience; to a follower, or junior (*kōhai*), paternal or brotherly guidance and leadership. With one's own fellows (*dōhai*)—age-mates, buddies, members of the same cohort—one normally feels freest of protocol; informal language and even first names can be used, one can be unbuttoned, let down one's hair, and not stand on ceremony. It is not that we could not understand these concepts—after all, we, too, have many relations that partake of that character—but that they represented a different way of perceiving those relations, and they implied different things about the nature of the relationship among the different elements. An American university student might recognize an alumnus as an "old grad"—to whom in Japanese the term *senpai* would correctly apply—but he would not feel the same range of obligations as implied by the Japanese term *senpai*. Therefore, while these Japanese concepts seem close to the English seniors-fellows–juniors, or some other variant of this sequence, they clearly meant much more.

Just as some Japanese words cannot be translated by a single English term, so there are some English concepts that cannot be translated by a single Japanese word. There is, for example, no good single word in Japanese to represent the English term "frustration." Depending upon context, this must be translated as *zasetsukan, shippai, shippaikan, ira-ira, tonza, kujiku koto, jirettai,* and so on. Each of these terms describes a different aspect of the total frustration experience. In English they are all covered by the same word; in Japanese they must be differentiated and covered by different words. But does the absence of a single comprehensive term for frustration in Japanese mean that the Japanese do not experience frustration? Obviously not. The language modality for expressing the experience, however, is totally different.

I have already mentioned insights about tense in connection with my first bête noire—*kashikomarimashita*. As we went more deeply into the language I was inclined at first to feel that the difference in tense pointed to some difference in the concept of the flow of time. Later on, I became less sure of this because I began to realize that neither was English—nor indeed any of the European languages I was familiar with—all that consistent about it. The divisions between past, present, and future are always vague and arbitrary, and how we happen to slice up the duration of time may easily vary—as a convention—in different languages. If the present is to be construed as this very moment, then what is this "moment": a microsecond, a second, a minute, today, this afternoon, this general period, the time it takes you to read this sentence, the present era of history? Or does it refer to the duration of an action or a thought or a mood, even though it is second-by-second encroaching on the future and second-by-second receding into the past, but unified by the psychological sense of the totality of the act or experience?

The problem then is how each language divides past, present, and future as grammatical categories requiring explicit expression in correct utterances. In Japanese, the so-called past tense is more accurately an affirmative form, and because it is emphatically affirmative, it often has the sense of completed action. In the case of *kushikomarimashita* and the very polite "thank you" (*arigatō gozaimashita*), the past tense intensifies the strong affirmative sense, thereby making the utterance politer or, more accurately, more deferential. But consider the following sequence:

You have to do that (*Kō shite yaranakiya dame da yo*).
Okay, okay (literally, "I understood, I understood"; *Wakatta, wakatta*).

He is not saying that he understood in the past, but rather emphatically that he fully understands (and perhaps does not need further pushing on the subject). The late Sir George Sansom in his unjustly neglected masterpiece, *A Historical Grammar of Japanese*, offered a striking example of a sentence, *roku-ji ni kaikanshiki owaru*, that can be translated as "the ceremony ends at six," or as "the ceremony ended at six," or as "the ceremony will end at six."

Another common type of example that we had to learn to cope with may be seen in the phrase "he went out when the cock crowed." But in Japanese, it is literally, "he went out when the cock crows" (*niwatori no naku toki ni dekaketa*). The word "crows" is in the present tense (or more accurately in the conclusive-attributive), but it refers to the past. The tense is indicated by the total context, not by the specific verb form.

The same kind of problem arises with regard to the future: does it start one instant in advance of the present instance, or does it start later? Both in English and in Japanese one can say something like, "I am going to the theater tonight" (*konban gekijō ni iku*), and in both cases, although the present tense is being used, it clearly refers to a future event. Does this mean that the speaker can feel certain about the future, or does it mean that his willing the future is a guarantee that the future will come?

But in Japanese it is also possible to have a sentence that says, literally, "in the future, when I secured a job..." (*shōrai jūshoku o shita toki...*). Here, the past tense is being used to refer to a future event. How is this to be interpreted? Of course, in English, too, we can say "when I will have found a job," but this implies a future situation in which having found a job will be in the past.

It used to be a standing joke in our school that "Japanese has a past and a present, but it has no future." This proposition about tense, however, was often understood to mean that it was Japan that had no future, a statement that made sense during the war. Yet as far as grammatical form is concerned, this is, in a sense, true. One may say "write" (*kaku*), or "writing" (*kaite imasu*), for the present, and "wrote" (*kakimashita*) for the past. But for the future, one must use auxiliary expressions such as "probably" (*kaku darō*), or "should" (*kakimashō*). The "probably" form (*darō*) implies some uncertainty about the future—a notion of probability, that future events are not certain but only probable in varying degrees, "I shall probably write." The "should" (*kakimashō*) form is hortatory and implies the necessity of human will to bring about the future.

But this is also true of English. The future forms require the auxiliary verbs "will" and "shall." "I will write," or "I shall write." The "will" implies human volition to bring the future event into existence, and the "shall" implies obligation, "It must be done." Both Japanese and English (and German) in this way differ from Spanish, French, and Italian, which have a real

94

future conjugation of the verb: in French, *j'écrirai*; in Spanish, *escribiré*.

These differences imply alternate ways of looking at the future, or alternate philosophies of the future, although whether in fact people actually perceive the implications of these in that way or not is still an open question to me. But despite certain similarities between English and Japanese in the construction of a future tense—or perhaps future "form" rather than "tense," is more correct—they certainly differ in how they divide the flow of time. In English it is more often necessary to be reasonably specific about time than in Japanese, and we were constantly running into examples of this, as in the case of *kashikomarimashita.* Since the Meiji period, however, and particularly since the end of World War II, Japanese has been so influenced by Western language and culture that tense usage gradually seems to be approaching the Western form.

As we proceeded to more advanced levels of the language, reaching farther into conceptual ranges, the differences between Japanese and English became increasingly revelatory. One could not simply translate from one language to another; one had to interpret. The words that had to be used were rarely exactly the same in the two languages. Any word, even the most apparently concrete, in any language, is in reality a complex of meanings. This might best be visualized as a circle, within which a range of related meanings is incorporated. The circle may be large, or it may be small, but the problem is that the circle of meaning in Japanese may not completely overlap the English circle.

In every language, most words, apart from those that tag specific objects or that denote rigidly defined mathematical or scientific terms, have a central core of meaning and a penumbra of associated meanings and affect. Sometimes the penumbra is narrow and sometimes it is broad. Among the languages that are historically related and have developed in some degree of association with each other—such as the European languages under the influence of Greek and Latin as well as of

95

each other—there is a reasonable overlap. But among languages that are unrelated historically and that have had little direct relation with each other, both core and penumbra may be very differently located.

We know this even among closely related European languages. The Portuguese will insist that *saudade* cannot be translated into English, certainly not by a single word. Its emotional penumbra, the range of things it covers, is too different: it is not only nostalgia, not only homesickness, not only longing, but all of them plus the feeling of love, of ineffable "ahness." Similarly, we are told, we can never properly translate the Spanish *simpático* because, although the notion of "sympathy" may lie at the heart of it, it spreads over a different range of meaning from the English word. Undoubtedly this is true.

How much more difficult it is, then, to try to make English and Japanese words overlap exactly. In many cases it takes several English words to capture a single Japanese word; in other cases, the situation is reversed. We early came across the problem of *kokoro*, the simplest translation of which is "heart." Lafcadio Hearn had struggled over it for many years, in fact entitling one of his books *Kokoro*, which he finally concludes can best be defined by the English phrase "the heart of things."

Kokoro has an enormous range of meanings, which intersect variously with the English words heart, mind, soul, spirit, etc. Ultimately it refers to the human heart and, by extension, to many other attributes of the human spirit that in Japanese have come to be related to it. The English "mind" refers ultimately to the organ of human intellection. In many cases what is described as "mind" in English comes out as "heart" in Japanese (and sometimes as "belly," *hara*). In order to translate the English word "mind" into Japanese many different words have to be used, for example: *kokoro* ("heart"), *hara* ("belly"), *chi* ("intellect"), *risei* ("reason"), *zunō* ("brains"), *atama*, ("head"), *shōki* ("consciousness"), *iken* ("opinion"), *kibun* ("frame of mind"), *chinō* ("intellectual ability") *kimochi* ("feeling"), *kidate* ("disposition"), *konomi* ("liking"), *shikō* ("way of thinking"), *kibō* ("wish"), *kioku* ("remembrance"), *chūi* ("attention"), *ishiki* ("awareness"), *kangae* ("idea"), *ito* ("intention"), *ki* ("spirit"), *kuisō* ("reflection"), *kanjō* ("emotion").

If we were to start at the other end, with the word *kokoro*, we would find in the same way that it requires many different English words to express what can be expressed by *kokoro* in Japanese: heart, mind, spirit, mentality, soul, idea, thought, feeling, will, intention, design, desire, inclination, fancy, taste, mood, humor, frame of mind, suspicion.

What we learned was that the word *kokoro* is not exactly the same as the word "heart." They overlap to some extent, but there are many uses of the word *kokoro* in Japanese that cannot be translated as "heart" in English. Neither is it exactly the same as "mind"; there is some overlap, but not complete. We can visualize the relation of these terms roughly as follows:

(The shaded area indicates the areas of common meaning.) If we look at the word "mind," we can see in the same way that there is no exact Japanese equivalent.

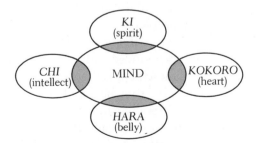

It is this kind of situation that makes it almost impossible to translate directly from the one language to the other; complex thoughts must be interpreted.

97

Chinese Ideographs

But it was our contact with *kanji,* the Chinese characters, that led us into an entirely different range of experiences. It is not simply a question of the ideographs; Chinese also uses them—after all they were originally designed to represent Chinese words. But there is a very important difference between the way *kanji* are used in Japanese and the way they are used in the original Chinese. In Chinese, each *kanji* has a single pronunciation (at least for each dialect of Chinese); that is, it is a single word. Because of the nature of the historical process by which Japanese ingested Chinese, a single character in Japanese has typically more than one pronunciation and more than one meaning. There is, for example, a character 生, which has the general sense of life, or living, but can be pronounced in at least twenty different ways and embraces a range of meanings that fit together nicely in Japanese, but that do not carry the same range of associations in English, or indeed in any other language.

The result is an experience that is entirely impossible in English, or indeed in any other nonideographic language: seeing and hearing on several different levels at the same time. When you see a *kanji* your mind runs over a number of alternative possible ways to pronounce it and a number of alternative meanings. When you hear a word, your mind runs over a number of alternative ways that it might be written. The mind thereby becomes more supple, it seems to me, more sensitive to language, to nuances, to possibilities. The name written 正道 , for example, can be pronounced either as Masamichi or as Seidō, and for most Japanese people it is exactly the same word. When hearing "Masamichi" they hear and see "Seidō" in their minds. It is a common experience to look at a visiting card that someone has just proffered and read off "———Masamichi?" and have him reply instantly, "Yes, ———Seidō."

The notion that Seidō and Masamichi can sound exactly the same is one that blows the mind of an American. But Japanese is full of these. You see 生 and you think *sei* ("life"), *shō* ("life"), jō ("life"), *ikiru* ("to live"), *fu* ("lawn"), *ikeru* ("to arrange flowers"), *nama* ("live," "raw"), *umu* ("to give birth"). You also sense many of the compounds to which the character lends itself, which ring slight variations on the common theme. So a single ideograph or a single word can be rich in associations, providing echoes and resonances that are entirely different from those in other languages.

This phenomenon, of course, provides the basis for punning, but also for unique poetic devices that are not possible in other languages. In a sense, we are all prisoners of our own language's particular syntactic structure. While this opens certain aesthetic experiences to us, it, at the same time, denies us others. Just as the Japanese speaker may never be able to experience the pleasures of rhyme unless he learns English, because his language does not lend itself to rhyme, so the English speaker will never be able to appreciate the "pivot words" (defined by Robert Brower and Earl Miner, *Japanese Court Poetry*, Stanford, Stanford University Press, 1961, p. 507) as a "rhetorical scheme of word play in which a series of sounds is so employed as to mean two or more things at once by different parsings. Take, for example, *nagame* used to mean "reverie" (*nagame*) and "long rains" (*naga-ame*). These, Miner tells us, "employ word plays in a kind of syntactic conceit, utilizing a single sequence of sounds to represent more than one word. . . . " They are, he adds, "as exciting to cope with as striking imagery." It is inherently impossible to transmit the experience that results from the perception of such relations between eye and ear and between one word and another on different levels. Once one has been able to do this, one has a new experience that is not possible in any other language, as, for example, the "broken or mixed allegory [which] has no counterpart in English . . . especially when the allegory of [some] poems . . . grows from images buried in pivot words and other complex verbal techniques."

Our own first attempt came at the most primitive level, the pun. It went as follows:

A: *Dō desu ka?*
B: *Iie, tetsu desu.*

Now, A's phrase normally has the meaning "How are you?" or "How are things going?" B, however, has elected to hear the phrase to mean something entirely different: "Is it copper?" The reason is that the sound *dō* ("how") brought to his mind's eye a Chinese character 銅, also pronounced *dō*, but having the meaning of "copper." Hence the reply is entirely appropriate, "No, it's iron." There is a sudden shift in the frame of reference, so that the reply refers back to a different frame from the one in which the question was asked. It was an example, feeble though it might be, of what Arthur Koestler, in his analysis of the logic of laughter in *The Act of Creation*, describes as "the delightful mental jolt of a sudden leap from one plane or associative context to another." But it did show that we had begun to internalize this process of seeing and hearing on two different levels. I therefore regard it as a significant step on our road to understanding Japanese.

Almost every day *kanji* provided one or another of us with such new experiences. "I think that learning *kanji* was the greatest part of the whole experience," one of my schoolmates, today a leading businessman, told me recently. "Even now, some thirty-five years later, I can still remember the excitement of discovery that came with mastering more and more *kanji*." Another schoolmate, William Arrowsmith, one of the world's distinguished classicists, translator of Greek and Latin, and now distinguished professor of classics at the Johns Hopkins University, was then eighteen, one of the youngest members of Company A. But he had already accumulated awesome credentials. At the age of sixteen or seventeen, he had been one of the founders of the famous literary journal *Chimaera* (after the war, the *Hudson Review*), and he had himself written a great deal, including poetry, literary criticism, and translation from the Latin and the Greek. It was hard to believe that at his tender age he could have developed such a wide acquaintanceship among classical scholars and writers. Japanese, however, did not interest him very much. He was doing it because he had been selected for Japanese language training in the Yale University Army Specialized Training Program, on account of his general linguistic ability. "It is not," he would say, "an interesting language." But the *kanji*, which were a fascinating intellectual puzzle, did intrigue him somewhat. "Can you imagine a language that has a special *kanji* for the Duke of Argyll's tea-tree?" he chortled to me one day. In the Rose-Innes dictionary, which was then our Bible, he had found the character 杞, which is defined as "*ki*, name of ancient province in China, [also read as] *kuko*, Duke of Argyll's tea-tree." For years that is what that particular word meant to me, until I later discovered additional renderings—"river willow," "Chinese matrimony vine"—in other dictionaries.

But, of course, memorizing large numbers of *kanji* was a hard job. Our seniors used to say that "the first thousand are the hardest; after that they come easy." And that was, it seems to me, the case. Because, as time went on, we began to internalize the patterns of the elements, both the two hundred and fourteen radicals and the hundreds of forms, and from them we came to see repetitive patterns. This gradually began to bring us close to the situation of the Japanese people, sometimes being able to read the sound of the character but not knowing its meaning and sometimes knowing the meaning without being able to pronounce it. For those of us who found this kind of excitement in *kanji*, the learning process was enormously facilitated.

The revelations continued apace: forms of compulsion—you *must* do such-and-such, for example. The prototypic Japanese form is, "If you don't do it, it will be bad." I found myself immediately forced to an awareness of many terms that I had entirely taken for granted in English. What does the difference between the English "must," "should," "ought to," "have to," and the Japanese form of "must" mean? The usual Japanese form does not quite say you *must* do such-and-such; it says that if you don't do it, it will be bad (*nakereba naranai*). The implication is that any person of normal sense will see the situation in the same way, that if it will not do *not* to do something, then effectively, it must be done. It suggested a common understanding of particular situations and an appeal to the individual's sociality or sense of obligation. This led then to much reflection on other concepts of compulsion, both in English and in the European languages. In Japanese, such phrases seemed on the whole to represent less compelling compulsion than their European counterparts and to rely more on the individual's sense of responsibility.

Given our stereotype of Japan as a class society in which compulsion was the norm, thus differing from the more egalitarian and individualistic West, where presumably the individual's good judgment was more to be relied upon than compulsion, this seemed strange. It also raised profound questions about a construction like, "I have to do." Did this imply a deep existential grounding of obligation in the individual as against what might be interpreted in the Japanese as the concept that obligation arises not constitutively from the inside, as it were, but from the network of social obligations within which the individual was imbedded?

I do not wish to suggest that I had discovered the proper answers, but rather to point out some of the kinds of questions that the study of Japanese brought to my own mind and, I am sure, to the minds of many of my fellow students.

Down the Line

By the end of that first year, we had all moved forward in our Japanese a good way, even though at our own individual paces. The first thousand *kanji* learned, some of the early trauma wore away. Among ourselves, we often took to speaking Japanese to each other. The language was so much in the forefront of our minds that it would automatically tumble out in conversations. Moreover, discussion in classroom, although well and good, was no longer sufficient to appease the appetites of some of us; so we supplemented the classroom work by talking to each other in Japanese. To some extent Japanese was like a new toy to play with. In spite of the intensiveness of our study, it was for most of us, I suspect, a very abstract thing. Aside from the BIJs and the few who had had combat experience in the Pacific, Japan was not the enemy but a locale where, it was implausibly rumored, people actually spoke this language. We used it as a secret code, since we could speak it in public with complete assurance that nobody would understand us. In Fort Mc-Clelland, Alabama, for example, where we were sent for two months of basic training after our first year of language study and before our last six-month stint at Fort Snelling, we used to speak to each other in Japanese so that the training cadre would not understand what we were saying. The cadre in any event had taken an instant dislike to our company of eggheads, college students, and unmistakably nonmilitary types. To taunt them, we often sang Japanese army or navy songs on our marches. After all, for most of us Japan was still pretty much of an abstraction rather than an enemy country. Nevertheless, the sight of a full American army company at the very height of the war against Japan swinging along to a Japanese navy song:

Behold! the Eastern Sea skies clear.
When the Rising Sun shines on high
There is justice in the universe,
Hope dances full of life,
Oh, Eight Great Islands!*

was a stunning one, and the cadre never quite knew what to do about it. One of our favorites, however, consisted simply of a series of sentences strung together from our early conversation lessons and sung to the tune of "We'll Build a Bungalow Big Enough for Two Underneath a Bamboo Tree."

Wakarimasu ka, wakarimasu ka

*Ōyashima, ancient, poetic name of Japan

103

Ryōriya de biiru o nomimasu ka?
Biiru o nomu.
Hayai hayai ayai yai. . .
Watakushi to issho ni nomi ni
Yopparai ni narimasu.

(Do you understand? do you understand?
Do you drink beer at the restaurant?
Drink beer.
Quick, quick, *ayai yai. . .*
Drinking beer with me,
We'll get drunk.)

After all this casual public use of Japanese in wartime America, where we were not likely to be understood, I can well remember the shock of first doing the same thing on the streets of Tokyo and suddenly realizing that it was really true: Japanese was a real language, not like ancient Greek or Latin, spoken by real people, not a private code for a small group of privileged American soldiers.

Closings

I ended up the year in Class One, having climbed all the way from the bottom of the heap to the top group. In that class there were seven men. Three of them left the army soon after the end of the war and never did become involved with Japan, in spite of the fact that they were all fine linguists. The other four, including myself, remained. Robert Spaulding is today professor of history, Oklahoma State University, and the author of the definitive work in English on the Imperial civil service examinations. Jack Seward, a lusty Texan always full of *joie de vivre,* who has been married several times—one of his wives was a Japanese model—and whose career has gone from government to business and writing, is the author of several books about Japan. William Dizer, general manager of Arco Chemicals, Asia, did his master's thesis on a style of provincial dramatic improvisation, the Hakata *niwakageki,* or "instant theater," is married to a Japanese, and lives in Tokyo.

The three who did not come to Japan have had diverse careers. One had his career in music; another went into his family's furniture business in Providence, Rhode Island; and the third, an accomplished pianist whom I always think of as playing George Gershwin, works in Washington.

On May 26, 1945, we graduated. The ceremonies were held in Rackham Lecture Hall of the University of Michigan and, as was customary, awards were handed out. Of the three "Instructors' Awards" recipients, only one remained involved with Japan. Nine men were given "honorable mentions." One of them committed suicide a few months later, four have had their major careers involved with Japan, one left the army to take over his family's business, and three I have not been able to trace.

The final award was to me: "Most Improved Student." I never did know how to take that: a compliment for having made the most progress, or a patronizing pat on the back for having made any progress at all from such a hopeless starting point. It was not a title that I could parade without hesitation.

The war came to its end while we were still on maneuvers at Fort McClelland. Our second day in the wilderness area near Morrisville, Alabama, the news about the atomic bomb dropped on Hiroshima suddenly passed through the company. The effect was electric—a sudden jolt of reality, and then the world looked entirely different. On the one hand, it meant that the end of the war was imminent and so the question of our own mission, for which we were training so hard, naturally arose: in that instant the raison d'être of what we were doing became unclear.

On the other hand, even though we had all been hoping for the defeat of Japan, and indeed that was precisely what we were working for, the atomic bomb seemed to change the rules of the game. One of our battalion commanders, a beefy Pacific combat veteran, rushed over, his face beaming with unrestrained delight. "I hope those bastards don't surrender. Then we can go ahead and atom bomb the whole goddamn country off the face of the earth. Kill every one of them, I say!" Some of our men agreed with this sentiment, and they were all beaming smiles from then on. But others were deeply disturbed. It was good that Japan had been defeated and perhaps the Bomb had to be used, but still, but still . . . The black-and-white morality of the very moment before had suddenly turned a dingy gray.

After this, the surrender came almost as an anticlimax, although we were naturally very excited when the news came to us back in camp. There was an air of uncertainty about everything. Now that the war was over, what would happen to our program? When would we get out of the army? What was the point of studying when the future was so unclear?

We arrived at Fort Snelling for the final portion of our language training with one hundred and sixty-five men. During the next month or two, about one-half of the men elected to leave the army. The other half decided to complete the language training and go on to further military service in the Occupation of Japan. There was something historically appropriate in the fact that our graduation and commissioning came precisely on December 7, 1945, the fourth anniversary of the Pacific War. By this time, there were only eighty-three of us left from the original Michigan group, including both officers and enlisted men. Seven Nisei, however, were also commissioned along with us, a sign of the changing times. We received an allowance of $250 to buy our officer uniforms, but I had been forgetful about having mine made. In haste, I bought a uniform that one of my commercially sharper buddies fobbed off on me; it did not fit very well. My career as an officer, therefore, started off appropriately enough with the uncomfortable feeling that my new officer's role would be as ill-fitting as my new officer's uniform.

Shortly thereafter, we set out on our path, not to the combat in the Pacific, for which we had been trained, but to occupied Japan.

V☆

ARRIVAL IN JAPAN

First Days

Fourteen days out from Seattle, our troopship, the U.S.S. *General Stewart*, reached Japanese waters. The first intimations of land came at about 5:30 in the morning. Soon the outlines of the Bōsō and the Miura peninsulas began to emerge, and we language officers stood almost rooted to the forward deck railings. The island of Ōshima was on our left as we headed for the entrance to Tokyo Bay, and we could see the city of Tateyama at the tip of the Bōsō Peninsula, the southeastern arm of Tokyo Bay. From that location, there is a famous view of Mount Fuji, but we could not see it as we had been hoping to because of the heavy sea fog. The old Japan hands had warned us that seeing Fuji on arrival or departure was a particularly significant omen. On our left was the Miura Peninsula, and when we passed the end of the peninsula we were inside Tokyo Bay.

After our fourteen days at sea, seeing another ship only once along the way, all of a sudden the waters came to life. Ships moved majestically down the sea lanes, giant gray men-of-war stood like iron sentinels pointing a baleful eye and guns on everything within range. Cutters and torpedo boats raced in

107

and out, and on every available surface the triumphant GI victory cry—"Kilroy Was Here"—was painted. The day was misted over, and the Bōsō side of the bay began to take on the aspect of a traditional black-and-white *sumie* ink drawing. My first impression, according to my diary, was of "mysterious promontories rising sheerly from the waters, a heavy brooding mist lying athwart them. The huge coil of mist lay from sea to mountains, like a cat's belly with its haunches sunk in the sea and its head dipping into mountain valleys behind the coastal ridge."

"Japan really *does* look like those pictures," someone remarked. Next came the city of Kisarazu on the right, and someone told us that it had been a jumping off place for kamikaze flyers during the last stages of the war. Then awesomely the old Imperial naval base of Yokosuka came into focus on our left. Yokohama was our destination.

Our first close-up view of Japan was a disappointment. All we could see were concrete works: piers, pilings, and docks—all in a dirty off-white—temporary wooden sheds; and a few permanent-looking administrative buildings. "There's nothing Oriental about this place at all," someone groaned. "It looks just like Milwaukee, Wisconsin." I was probably not the only one beginning to wonder whether all of Japan was going to be the same kind of experience—an Oriental Milwaukee. For all that we were not unrealistic and this was the land of the enemy, which we knew to be an industrial society, there lingered within deep layers of our consciousness a romantic image of Japan as a land of toy houses, delicate people in delicate kimono, temple bells, and pagodas. And, of course, Mount Fuji and geisha. I myself had not yet read Lafcadio Hearn, but many of the others had; and besides, the Lafcadio Hearn image of Japan had subtly permeated a great deal of the Western awareness of Japan.

The reality we encountered was not this, to say the least. The first "enemy" Japanese we encountered were dock workers. They were ill-clad, unkempt, and unshaven. Who started the ugly exchange I do not know, but the stevedores were begging

108

for cigarettes and we were tossing butts at them. It was not a
pleasant sight. Then somebody came up with the more amusing idea of throwing the butts so they would roll off the edge
and fall into the water. Every scramble brought shouts of approval and encouragement, and soon some of the men began to
place bets on who would succeed in catching the butts.

By the time we managed to get off the ship and set foot on
Japanese soil it was already nightfall. We started out in a convoy
of trucks, and at Yokohama Station we were transferred to a
train bound for Zama, a former Japanese Imperial Army base,
which was to be our intake camp. The cars were old and
beaten-up, broken windows patched with tape, wood, and cardboard, the seats straight-backed with a thin green plush covering the wooden backs. The night was cold, and we shivered
within. Every few minutes the train jolted to a stop and then sat
for ten or fifteen minutes. We shuttled back and forth, changed
locomotives every few miles, and stood on sidings for long
periods of time. We were all very eager, as can be imagined, to
get a glimpse of the "real Japan." But it was night, and the
countryside we stopped in was usually unlighted. Whenever the
train stopped, we were besieged by hundreds of people lining
the tracks, often in tatters or odds and ends of leftover Imperial
army uniforms, but mostly women in *mompe*, the compulsory
wartime baggy trousers, and loose overblouse, carrying infants
on their backs and begging for food, chocolate, cigarettes,
money, or anything else. "The children would reach up appeal-
ingly and cry *'purezento,'*" my diary notes. This was the first
time we had heard this word and it took us some time to figure
out that it was the English word "present." The sight was like
something out of Dostoyevsky's underground, and we language
officers did not know how to react to it.

Many of the other soldiers on the train were doing a land office black market business, selling cigarettes by the piece or by
the box, chocolate, and K-rations for amounts that seemed to
me enormous, or buying little trinkets and art objects. One
Nisei officer bought a large and pretty silk scarf for three packs

of cigarettes. Packs of cigarettes were being sold for fifteen yen apiece, which, at the official exchange rate of five yen to the dollar, meant three dollars. But a whole carton of cigarettes at that time cost us a dollar in the PX.

We language officers became more and more silent watching these transactions. But we were also eager to try out our hard-gained language, so whenever the train came to another of its innumerable stops and we were overrun by beggars and buyers, we began to strike up conversations. It was disheartening. Words passed back and forth, but there was no genuine contact. We also discovered that the standard polite forms we had learned at school were entirely inappropriate to use with little children and beggars.

Our first morning in the Zama camp, we woke up 7:30 A.M. of a gray, muddy day, finding ourselves not in a regular barracks but in a classroom that had been assigned to us for a billet. Our first military activity of the morning was an orientation lecture, a good part of which was devoted to persuading us to avoid Japanese women like the plague. "Our sampling of Japanese women indicates a VD rate of 90 percent," the medical officer told us, "with 50 percent having more than one venereal disease."

Although by this time we had been technically on Japanese soil for the better part of a day, since we were still locked away in an army camp, we felt on the edge, as it were, not quite in. The Japanese we saw were menials, employed to do all the chores that enlisted men dislike most—making beds, sweeping, KP. They wore a weird combination of discarded army clothing, whether American or Japanese, combined with remnants of the wardrobe of some time long past. For many of the GIs, the incongruity of underwear showing through oversized jackets and balloon trousers, secured with Japanese army puttees, from the bottom of which protruded straw sandals or wooden clogs, was a matter for high glee. Just to see this bizarre costume was to confirm the disposition they already had to feel superior. The Japanese we saw in the camps were a runty, sad-looking lot, obsequious, desperately trying to understand the alien English spoken all around them, anxious to hang on to these jobs in order to keep their families afloat.

For the first time, we began to realize what the abstract statistical notion of "Japan's postwar food shortage" really meant. I noted in my diary that first day: "About twenty women and numberless children were around back of the mess hall grubbing in GI trash cans and begging slops. A few of us brought out a little food, bread, and so on. But it's only a drop in the bucket. The whole business is hopeless. Japan simply cannot be fed from the leavings of army posts. Larry and I went out to take some pictures. It was pitiable. The insult to their dignity of our taking pictures of their plight was hard for them to bear. Every time we turned our cameras at them, they scattered like startled sheep, running in all directions away from the humiliation of the lens. But the need for handouts struggled against their reticence, and they went ahead anyway. Nisei soldiers, rather grim-faced, were the ones handing out the slops. The people carried tin cans, oil cans, buckets, or other containers to the door of the kitchen, and the GIs were filling them with our leftovers.

"The women, many with children on their backs, in a variety of costumes ranging from bright kimono to *mompe*, wearing boots, split-toe socks, clogs, and some even shoeless, were dignified. Young pretty wives, old white-haired grandmothers, all reduced to begging for our scraps. The Nisei boys told me that when they arrived four days ago, they found these women picking over the greasy liquid trash in the cans for edible bits. They were so horrified that they organized this regular handout. 'At least these are clean leftovers,' they said. They were pretty hard hit by the whole business. One woman, they told me, walked three miles each way every day to pick up some food. There seems to be absolutely no food around. One old gal who had garnered some bread went around stuffing bits into the mouths of the babies on their mothers' backs. And the people here are lucky. What if there were no army camp?"

By the next afternoon, however, we had completed most of our formalities and several of us set out to Tokyo for our first sight of the capital city of our conquered enemy. The electric train was jammed with people as it rattled from station to station. Many were carrying large packs, on their backs or shoulders, filled with rice or other foods they had been able to buy from farmers out in the countryside.

The smell of the packed bodies had an acrid quality that reminded me of a crowded bus in provincial Mexico. Something I had read in Pierre Loti about his little love nest in Nagasaki came to mind: "... a strange odor mingles with the musk and the lotus—an odor essential to Japan, to the yellow race, belonging to the soil or emanating from the venerable woodwork ... almost an odor of wild beast." It is true that the Japanese have a characteristic odor. But so have Westerners, I realized. An old term for something that "seems Western" is *bata-kusai*, that is, "smelling of butter." This smell undoubtedly comes from our diet, which includes a large amount of meat and dairy products. Today, now that the Japanese diet has become somewhat Westernized—with meat, bread, butter, cheese, and milk—the Japanese smell, like Japanese culture and the Japanese economy, has probably become more like the Western one. Of course, in our packed train, the smell was special; this was postwar Japan, miserable and short of food, soap, and decent clothes.

As we pushed our way into the mass of bodies, they gave way reluctantly, as if in response to an unspoken command. It was agreeable to find some room for standing or sitting, but it was hard to think of oneself as a conqueror worthy of such submissiveness. These thoughts quickly gave way, however, to an awareness that the passengers had somehow managed to redefine the situation: we were not conquerors, but rather honored guests. On these terms, it was much easier to accept the privileges, not as obsequiousness, but as civilized hospitality.

Looking at this train full of Japanese, I felt a *frisson* of excite-

112

ment go through me, partly because I was going to have to use this language for real, not as a school subject. I carefully rehearsed several phrases of varying degrees of politeness, undecided as to what level would be appropriate under the circumstances. What came out, I am not sure, but the carefully selected words directed to my neighbor strap-hanger drew a response, much to my surprise. I assayed an answer, and before I knew it we were actually launched on a conversation: my first genuine Japanese conversation with a genuine Japanese in Japan.

My neighbor, it turned out, was a retired diplomat, now an executive in an electrical machinery company. He had all the proper élite credentials—Tokyo University, Faculty of Law —and had spent much of his career in, of all places, Latin America. When he learned that I had spent a year in Mexico and that I spoke Spanish, he insisted upon switching from Japanese to Spanish. To my utter bafflement, we spent the remainder of the trip, hanging onto our straps as the train shook us up thoroughly on the way to Tokyo, speaking Spanish.

We walked along the main street that fronts the Imperial moat, called "Avenue A" by the Occupation, he briskly and I haltingly, because I was trying to take in Japan as we continued to talk about Latin America in Spanish. Suddenly he stopped, as if we had reached our destination. "The Imperial Theater," he told me, drawing me firmly through a long queue into the lobby of the theater that suddenly appeared before us. A Kabuki performance was under way. Although the theater was full and all seats taken, my forceful host marched up to the manager and requested a box for the American soldier. Without the slightest hesitation, a small party was cleaned out of a box and we were installed. The play was the classic *Momijigari*, "The Maple-Viewing Party," and as I sat dazzled by the great pine tree in the center of the stage, the costumes looking as if some of our Army Intensive Japanese Language School movies had suddenly come to life, and by the strange but exciting pitch of the voices, he began to explain and to interpret for me—in

113

Spanish. Scarcely listening to his words, nor to the words on the stage, few of which even reached me through the wall of Spanish, I was especially impressed by the music. The sudden cracking of wooden blocks on the floor of the stage, the jerky strumming of the three-stringed guitar, the shamisen, moving up rapidly to great climaxes of speed and volume, the chanting of the chorus, the elusive, yet somehow inevitable, pacing of music, words, and action.

"And now let me take you to the Ginza," my guide said, leading me out of the magical dark into the bright glare of day, whereupon I finally pulled myself together and then outgamed him with my most elegant Spanish thrust-riposte of politeness until he finally backed down from the engagement. In both Spanish and Japanese, politeness is a very powerful weapon of aggression. Stendhal has somewhere said that the mark of the French aristocrat is the ability to flatter outrageously and without limit. Apologizing and thanking my host profusely, I graciously accepted his calling card, the *meishi*—my first experience of this Japanese custom—and then made my escape.

Free of my all too friendly guide, I started to look over this city that I seemed to have spent so much of my life preparing to see. The broad avenue fronting the Imperial moat was lined with seedy, but durable buildings, of an average height of six stories. Nearby was General MacArthur's headquarters, the reconverted Dai-Ichi (Number One) Insurance Building, its rectangular columns rising five floors and scrubbed to a respectable gray-white. Crowds lined the street across the entrance, held back with no effort by stunning MPs, tall and massive, trimmed with white gloves and shoulder ornaments, as if stamped from some gigantic cookie cutter. As General MacArthur stepped through the great portals of the Dai-Ichi Building to walk his few carefully staged steps to the waiting black Cadillac, a murmur rippled through the crowd, some older people bowing their heads reverently as they would to the emperor of Japan, younger people watching with frank curiosity, American soldiers saluting, a few Japanese cheering modestly. Many had a

114

look I was to get to know very well later on, a peculiar half-smile that looked as if it could turn into a scowl or a full smile, depending on the cue they received.

The Hibiya Crossing in central Tokyo was another sideshow—this time, even for American soldiers. Gigantic American MPs, accoutred in costumes worthy of a Latin American general and moving with gestures that recalled the goose step or the jerking of marionettes, were directing the traffic. Japanese policemen, about half their size, most of them in ill-fitting uniforms, tried to imitate their movements. While one group stood in the middle of the street at work, another team waited on the curb for its turn. As soon as the first was exhausted by its pedagogical efforts, the other took over. Occasionally a Japanese traffic cop would get the rhythm and for a moment even outdo his American mentor, with more exaggerated gestures or higher leaping into the air, whereupon the roar of laughter could be heard even over the traffic. While most of the American soldiers were amused, it seemed to me that for many Japanese the laugh was one of embarrassment. Were they thinking that Japanese were being made fools of, or acting like fools; that this was to be the pattern of their lives, to be educated in the ways of democracy by American soldiers?

Late in the afternoon, I decided to launch myself on the city and see what would happen. First, I went to the NYK Building, the headquarters of Japan's largest steamship company. It had been turned into an officer's billet and many members of our company who had earlier cleared the Zama red tape were already installed. The Tokyo Marine Insurance Building across the way still stood as a façade, but it had been gutted by a bomb and only one or two floors were in use. A friend secured a jeep from the motor pool and we set out to look for a girl he had met a few nights before. We had the address, but we had no map of Tokyo, either in our pockets or in our heads.

The scene was fantastic. For the first time, we realized what the cold figures meant, that 60 percent of the land surface of Tokyo had been destroyed by bombing. The immediate area of

General MacArthur's headquarters was lined with tattered, but still serviceable, buildings. A few blocks away, however, one entered upon a veritable desert.

The American bombing, it will be recalled, was mainly of the incendiary type; very little of the demolition type had been used. Traditional Japanese buildings were flimsy structures of wood and paper, and they burned to the ground almost without trace. You could pass through bombed areas and hardly realize that they had been other than a wilderness before. Unlike the bombed-out European cities, with their jagged wounds of broken steel, concrete, and brick, which left the tortured landscapes we all came to know from postwar movies, the Japanese houses had burned completely, leaving no trace, like a considerate old lady expiring quietly and without fuss, so as not to cause trouble to others. For miles on end, all that was left standing were the blocky godowns, in which families of substance placed their valuables, and chimneys, marking where bathhouses and other public structures had stood. Since these godowns were usually built of heavy materials several feet thick and secured with massive iron locks, ordinary fire bombs did not touch them. The desolation, punctuated by the undamaged godowns, seemed like some exotic new form of city planning. People who were fortunate enough to have a godown were able to move into it, small though it might be, when their houses had burned down.

After thinking for many years that I was the only one to make this observation, I ran across the following entry in the journal of Erwin Baelz, a German who had served for some years as a medical consultant for the Imperial Household. Dated December 1, 1876, just after Tokyo's devastating fire of November 30, it notes:

> Even the site of the conflagration, vast though it is, does not look so hopeless as a burned-out quarter of a European town. A foreigner, brought here for the first time, would scarcely realize what had happened. . . . There are still build-

ings . . . on the ground. . . . These stalwarts that remain are the 'fireproof godowns,' the *kura*, of which every merchant or big shopkeeper has several, and almost every reasonably well-to-do person at least one. . . . It is they which give the burned areas so peculiar a stamp. Of the real dwelling-houses, built of wood, nothing remains beyond broken tiles. You do not find in Japan, as after a great fire in a Western town, bare, blackened walls still rising heavenward, the charred skeletons of once fine buildings; there are no fragments of household utensils, half-used lumps of metal, broken and twisted stove and fireplace—nothing, nothing.

Because of the destruction, practically all landmarks were down, and we found it almost impossible to follow the directions that we frequently had to ask for to lead us to our destination. Finally we discovered the trick: follow a trail of neighborhood police stations (*kōban*). We plotted a line from where we were to where we wanted to go and asked at every one of these little neighborhood police boxes for instructions on how to reach the next police box on the path. In this way, we saw much of the inner part of Tokyo that lay between the Imperial moat and the line formed by the loop line of the elevated railway.

Leaving my friends to whatever their diversions might be that night, I set out for a walk and ran across another army buddy who had already been in Tokyo for a month or two. "There are a lot of interesting places around Shinagawa," he volunteered, and so we took the elevated train to Shinagawa Station. The Shinagawa area was at that time the center for black troops of, I believe, the Twenty-fourth Division. After a few minutes' walk through the streets, we decided it was too rough for us. So we took the train back to town, getting off at the Yūrakuchō Station.

As we came to one of the exit turnstiles we saw a startling scene. Two groups of about fifteen men each stood on opposite sides of the entryway holding baseball bats, clubs, and a variety of other handy weapons. At the moment we passed through the turnstile into the clearing, they were frozen in that tense stillness that one sees in samurai movies the moment before the great swordsman makes his perfect swing, heel and ball of the foot sliding millimicrometers to shift the balance more favorably, the weaponed arms inching almost imperceptibly to a more advantageous position for a decisive stroke. One small man, in plus fours and wispily moustached, had just dashed back from a position too close to the enemy to his own safer side. The panorama remained frozen a moment and then, as they caught sight of our second lieutenant bars, they straightened up and lowered their weapons. "Let's get out of here," my more knowledgeable companion whispered fiercely, grabbing my arm near the elbow. "Gang fight." We walked slowly across the stage, all eyes following us from unmoved faces. As we stepped through the exit to the outside, a shout went up followed by the clear thwack of bats beating other bats, heads, arms, and walls. Right after the war, Koreans had moved into the black market and the rackets in force, often having to muscle out Japanese gangs that had been in control. What we had just witnessed was one small skirmish in that war. I don't know who won that time.

It was now about 11 P.M., and my friend, who had already been in Japan long enough to have lost some of his initial sense of wonder, decided to go back to his billet to sleep. But I was still too wide awake, so I went on, walking down from the Yūrakuchō Station through the warren of little shops, open-air stalls, and drinking and eating establishments toward the Sukiyabashi corner and then down toward the heart of Tokyo's downtown district, the Ginza's fourth block. One of the words that had intrigued me in language school was *ginbura*. It was a typical example of Japanese word-play. The first syllable, *gin*, comes from the word "Ginza," the second, *bura*, comes from the duplicating word *bura-bura*, which means "to stroll, or roam, or wander unhurriedly." Together they mean "taking a stroll on the Ginza." I had always wanted to experience it. It was late, of course, and it was still not long after the end of the war, but there were people wandering about sufficiently aimlessly, it seemed to me, to qualify for my image of what *ginbura* should be. Some months later, when living conditions had much improved, I went one Sunday and then really discovered what it meant.

I chatted happily with everyone willing to exchange conversation with me, but I found that my uniform was both an advantage and a curse. I was conspicuous as I had never before been in my life, even among the Tarahumara Indians in Mexico, and I was not prepared for the hordes of children in tatters running around begging and offering to shine shoes, the pimps and the tarts for whom an American soldier was a natural target, the constant staring, and, at the slightest word of Japanese dropped from my mouth, the goggling to which I was subjected. It was not until about 2:30 in the morning that I arrived back at the NYK Building for my first Tokyo slumber.

The Conquest of Japan

Other men, other encounters. Let me relate only two. A friend of mine was commanding officer of a unit sent up to prepare the way for General MacArthur's formal arrival. "That meant," he told me, "to take over Tokyo. Imagine how that sounded to a bunch of GIs fresh from combat!" His unit, a part of the First Cavalry Division, had been in some of the bitterest fighting in Okinawa. They arrived in Yokohama peacefully, but with their combat habits still intact. Every man was heavily armed, grenades hanging in clusters like grapes.

After lining up outside the dock area for their transportation to Tokyo, they finally turned their attention to the scene before them. They were staggered: hundreds of Japanese civilians were waiting for them on the edge of the road, waving American flags hastily made up for the occasion. The thin red line wavered in confusion, some guards slipping, some hands tightening on the rifle stocks.

119

"We suspected a trick," my friend told me. "We knew there were three million armed Japanese troops on the home islands, and after our experience on Okinawa, how could we be sure this was not an ambush?" They trudged forward, bayoneted rifles held at the ready, and marched straight into the crowd of old men, women, and children. While the soldiers were being cheered and loaded with presents of bits of silk cloth, brocade, swords, or any other treasures still around after four years of war, the officers were met by a formal reception committee.

The crowd opened a path for them, and they saw a fleet of aging automobiles, almost all charcoal burners, waiting with official drivers to take them to Tokyo. But they were still suspicious, so they refused the cars and set off on the road to Tokyo in the jeeps they had brought along with them. The fleet of cars trailed behind them all the way in a long procession.

Upon their arrival in Tokyo, they set about their mission, taking over the Imperial Hotel, the American Embassy, the Dai-Ichi Insurance Building, and some others to be used by the Occupation. For their own quarters, they took over an elementary school, staked out a perimeter, and posted sentries. The first night they were approached by Japanese offering to guide them to bordellos that had been set up by the Japanese government in the hope that they would keep the American troops away from "respectable" women. They refused the offer and shut themselves in. The next night, however, there having been no unpleasant incidents during the course of the day, several of them decided to go out on the town. "There we were," my friend recalled, "a handful of combat veterans, probably the only American soldiers in Tokyo on that day, still in battle fatigues and carrying sidearms. Before the night was over we were all on our own, individually or in small groups. We walked the streets of the Ginza, shopping, drinking in bars, eating in restaurants, picking up girls. The next morning, every man was accounted for; there had not been one single unpleasant incident. The boys were loaded with souvenirs, and they had had the time of their lives. From then on, nobody carried sidearms again." Several days later, the first regular Occupation troops began to arrive.

Arthur Tiedeman, now professor of history and dean of the social sciences at the City University of New York, but then a language officer, also arrived in Japan before the formal surrender. His hospital ship from the Philippines docked in Yokohama on August 31. But they were not the first: some army units and the Fourth Marines had already landed on August 28 and General Eichelberger the day before. Yokohama headquarters were established in the prefectural government office, and they were ordered to carry their carbines with them when they went into the streets. "I did so," he recalls, "but I did not carry any ammunition along." What struck him was how quiet everything was. There were no Japanese soldiers, only some elderly and scruffy policemen. All of a sudden there was an alarming noise, as if large numbers of people were on the move. The noise, it turned out, was not in any way hostile. It was the sound of the crowd of movie-goers leaving the nearby movie house.

My own encounter was later than this, and many things had changed. But for the first year or so after the war, most of the Americans who came to Japan went through an evolution basically similar to the one experienced by my friend and his combat unit in late August 1945. The collective American image of Japan was of a race of beetle-browed, snaggle-toothed, squat men, treacherous, cruel, clannish, dangerously cunning in battle, and contemptuous of life—their own as well as others'. A very good example may be seen in the wartime illustrations by cartoonist Milton Caniff, the creator of "Terry and the Pirates," on "How to Spot a Jap," which was widely distributed by the United China Relief Committee (see p. 122).

But these attitudes dissolved almost immediately on contact with Japan. It was fascinating to watch the process at work among newly arrived GIs fresh out of the foxholes of Okinawa, their eyes bloodshot, their quaint battle trophies of Japanese teeth dangling from their belts like Indian scalps, out for blood.

121

HOW TO SPOT A JAP

HERE ARE TWO MEN JUST PICKED UP BY A PATROL...THE FIRST THING TO CONSIDER IS APPEARANCE...THE CHINESE IS "**C**"... THE JAP IS "**J**." NOTICE THAT **C** IS ABOUT THE SIZE OF AN AVERAGE AMERICAN; **J** IS SHORTER—AND LOOKS AS IF HIS LEGS ARE JOINED DIRECTLY TO HIS CHEST!...

C IS DULL BRONZE IN COLOR—WHILE **J** IS LIGHTER—MORE ON THE LEMON-YELLOW SIDE. **C**'S EYES ARE SET LIKE ANY EUROPEAN'S OR AMERICAN'S—BUT HAVE A MARKED <u>SQUINT</u>...**J** HAS EYES SLANTED TOWARD HIS NOSE...

THE CHINESE HAS A SMOOTH FACE...THE JAP RUNS TO HAIR...LOOK AT THEIR PROFILES AND TEETH...**C** USUALLY HAS EVENLY SET CHOPPERS—**J** HAS BUCK TEETH...THE CHINESE SMILES EASILY—THE JAP USUALLY EXPECTS TO BE SHOT...AND IS VERY UNHAPPY ABOUT THE WHOLE THING... ESPECIALLY IF HE IS AN OFFICER!

YOU MAY FIND JAPS AMONG ANY ORIENTAL CIVILIAN GROUP...THAT IS A FAVORITE INFILTRATION TRICK...MAKE YOUR MAN WALK...THE CHINESE STRIDES...THE JAP SHUFFLES (BUT HE MAY BE CLEVER ENOUGH TO FAKE THE STRIDE)...MAKE HIM REMOVE HIS SOCKS AND SHOES, IF ANY...

THE CHINESE AND OTHER ASIATICS HAVE FAIRLY NORMAL FEET...THE JAP WORE A WOODEN SANDAL ("GETA") BEFORE HE WAS ISSUED ARMY SHOES...HE WILL USUALLY HAVE A WIDE SPACE BETWEEN THE FIRST AND SECOND TOES...OFTEN CALLOUSED FROM THE LEATHER STRAP THAT HELD THE "GETA" TO HIS FOOT...

TO SUM IT UP, SPOTTING A JAP DEPENDS UPON THREE THINGS. 1. <u>APPEARANCE</u> 2. <u>FEET</u> 3. <u>PRONUNCIATION</u>

HE CAN'T PRONOUNCE OUR LIQUID "L"... HISSES ON ANY "S" SOUND.

ALMOST NO WAIST-LINE

STOCKY BUILD

SHORT, SQUAT, FAIRLY HEAVY BEARD...LEMON-YELLOW SKIN, SLANTED EYES.

G-STRING

WIDE SPACE BETWEEN FIRST AND SECOND TOES...CALLOUS ON THE WEB

Within days the hard eyes had softened, and they were busy sampling Japanese liquor, girls, and tatami rooms, bumping their heads on the low doorways, clumsily uncrossing their chopsticks, awkwardly fumbling their combat boots as they went in and out of Japanese houses. When the next batch of newcomers arrived, stiff with their own undissolved suspicions, the veterans of a week before would look at them with understanding eyes and say, "Just wait for a week or so."

While the language officers did not start out with quite the same load of suspicions and stereotypes, the fundamental process was quite similar.

Assignment in Fukuoka

My group of language officers was held in Tokyo for several weeks awaiting our permanent assignment. In our eyes, the most desirable assignment was Tokyo itself, the center of the Occupation and the center of the country. Despite the devastation and the misery, it was still a vital center bubbling with life. Next in order of desirability was the Kansai area—Kyoto for the serious students of Japanese culture and Osaka or Kobe for the others. Third down the line was Fukuoka, one of Japan's main cities but which at that point appeared to us the remotest of provinces. Beyond that came outer darkness: Korea. For language officers who had invested so much of their emotions and lives in the study of Japanese, to be sent to Korea seemed a fate worse than death.

Because of the ferocity of the competition for Tokyo, the final decision was made by the drawing of lots. I drew Fukuoka, and although I was disheartened not to make Tokyo, at least I could breathe a sigh of relief that it had not been Korea, as happened to one of my ex-roommates. Let me make it clear that our attitude about Korea was not the result of any anti-Korean sentiment on our part. In the abstract all of us had great sympathy for the Koreans, whom we looked upon as victims of Japanese imperialism. It was only that after all of the time we had spent on Japanese we were desperate to put that effort to work. We had also heard, through the military rumor networks, that Korea of late 1945 and early 1946 was a very dismal place to be posted, and this did not make the Korean detour more appetizing. After a few days, I picked up my assignment to the Civil Censorship Detachment in Fukuoka and, along with five other officers, set out for my new assignment.

Our progress to Fukuoka was a grim reminder, if we still needed any after what we had already seen in Tokyo, that Japan was a devastated country filled with desperately suffering people, not just a place for American language officers to practice their newly learned Japanese. The train made a short stop in Hiroshima, and there was nothing standing between the station and the cracked chimneys of Hiroshima University on the hills except for the twisted carcass of a department store which had been of ferroconcrete construction. It was hard to believe that anything had happened here. Everything had burned down so completely that it required an act of the imagination to remember that there had once been a city here. But still the forsythia was blooming and from the train we could see people shuffling in the vast emptiness, here and there throwing up shelters, cultivating vegetable patches, and otherwise going about the business of daily life to the extent that the devastation permitted.

The ride was a long one. I am not sure exactly how long, but at least thirty hours, and we arrived at the station in the middle of the night. The platform was crowded with thousands of people. Fukuoka was then a transfer point for Japanese being repatriated from the mainland of Asia and for Koreans being shipped to Korea from Japan. From Fukuoka the returnees would head their respective ways home if they had one, or wherever else it was that they were going if they did not. Those who had tickets were lucky, even though the trains were so jammed that there was no place to sit down, much less to stretch out. Others had to wait for days on end even to secure a ticket. These were tired, defeated, and dispirited people.

A group of about four very drunken Australian soldiers were

amusing themselves by forcing the crowds on the platform to line up and to bow to them as they walked back and forth. It was appalling. Old men and ladies, bone-weary, along with all the rest of the returnees, were obliged to remain standing up and bow every time an Australian soldier passed in front of them. In the foggy light of the station platform, all sounds curiously muted, the capering red-faced Australians and the waves of bowing returnees were an eerie sight, and we were outraged. Should we go in and break it up? This would surely mean a fight with some very nasty drunken Australians. Or should we look for the MPs? Just then some MPs came into view, dismounted from their motorcycles, and, as soon as they made their appearance on the platform, the Australians took off and fled the scene. The MPs went after them, but whether they caught up with them or not, we never did learn.

Since we were language officers, our primary task was to apply our knowledge of Japanese to the needs of the Occupation. But as of the end of our training, most of us were just at the threshold from which we could either move forward, with a lot of hard practice, or fall back. A few were over the threshold, a few just short of it.

What determined whether we advanced or not was our subsequent experiences. Many of the language officers were assigned positions that gave them little occasion to use their Japanese. They tended to fall back instead of advancing. In ATIS (Allied Translation and Interpreting Service), for example, where many of our classmates were assigned, the practice was to put the language officer in charge of a team of Nisei or Japanese translators with whom he could deal in English. Many of the language school graduates, therefore, did not get the chance to sharpen their school-learned Japanese in real life situations and, as a result, their Japanese deteriorated badly. Others were immediately placed in positions that required them to use their language. I was one of the lucky ones.

Fukuoka had not been considered a choice assignment. At that time its command was in process of being transferred from the Fifth Marine Amphibious Corps to the Thirty-second (Red Arrow) Army Division. Among the military down in provincial Fukuoka there was none of the gentility of the GHQ types up in Tokyo. The marines had been rough and tough; not only did their legacy remain behind, but many marines themselves also remained during the early part of my stay. The Thirty-second Division had only a marginally better reputation, although it did not improve with the fairly frequent battles that broke out between its white and black troops in the bars, nightclubs, geisha houses, and houses of prostitution. In addition, there were the Australians who carried a heavy animus against the Japanese and had even fewer inhibitions than American combat veterans about displaying it. All of our group had wanted to be in Tokyo, where the action was, or at least in Osaka, which offered the delights of a large city and was within reachable distance of Kyoto and Kobe.

To our surprise, however, Fukuoka turned out to be a great assignment—not the work itself, but the general situation. The Civil Censorship Detachment (CCD), Telecommunications, to which we were assigned, was under the control of the navy, either because the navy was presumed to have more expertise in communications than the army or, as seems more likely, as a grudging concession of command to a brother service. There were about twelve of us—six army language officers, the rest navy officers. The work consisted of monitoring the flow of cable and telephone between Japan and Korea.

Our naval commander had the quaint idea that since we were language officers we should do all the monitoring of telephones and the reading of cables by ourselves. He refused to use Nisei or Japanese. Partly this was because he personally did not trust the Japanese. (Later on, however, he did a one-hundred-and-eighty-degree turnabout and ended up making his living in Japan, married to a Japanese woman.) Partly, it was simply a continuation into the Occupation of the navy's policy toward Japanese-Americans. Nevertheless, it worked to our benefit.

126

The job was boring: it is hard to imagine anything more uninteresting than reading cables or listening in on hard-to-understand telephone conversations. But it did a world of good for our Japanese. It forced us to use our Japanese from the very first day, and the result was that on average we did better than most of our classmates.

What the purpose of this was, we were never entirely sure. It seemed very unlikely that we would catch any spies that way. But perhaps we did turn up some useful information on economic matters, black marketing, violations of the law, and possibly on potential war criminals. To one of our navy language officer predecessors, it was "makework—W.P.A. in uniform."* Although I myself was never quite sure what our mission was, it was his belief that "Our function . . . was to keep the big, bad Mitsui and Mitsubishi *zaibatsu* [cartels] from retaining control over their Korean subsidiaries by any mysterious conspiracy, after their representatives in Korea had been repatriated to Japan." What did we accomplish? On the telephones, nothing, he concludes, because the language officers could not understand what was being said. "As for telegraphs, we could and did annoy individual Japanese trying to sell their property in Seoul to their Korean friends and associates."

Learning about Japan

Whatever the final verdict of history may be, all in all, it would be hard to imagine a better first posting for language officers lusting to use their language. Our billet was a small Japanese-style inn, the Ueno, in the heart of the old merchants quarter of Gofukuchō, or "Clothing Street." Nearby, there was a tiny Shinto shrine that sat in its own park.

The inn was exactly large enough for our group, and so we

*Martin Bronfenbrenner, now Kenan Professor of Economics at Duke University, in his charming collection of tales of the Occupation: *Tomioka Stories—From the Japanese Occupation*, Hicksville, N.Y., Exposition Press, 1975, pp. 131–32.

had it all to ourselves. From there we could walk to our work and also to the mess hall where we usually had our meals. We could also feel some of the rhythms of Japan—wooden clogs clacking on the pavements, the early morning song of the vendor of the Japanese delicacy, fermented soy beans (*nattō*), the clatter of shop-front shutters, the opening and closing of the storm shutters, the bustle of householders sweeping the streets, the stumbling shuffle of drunks returning from a party.

Because of my academic background, I made a point of having contact with Japanese academics. At Kyushu University (formerly, Kyushu Imperial University), I met one of Japan's leading (and then very scarce) sociologists, Professor Kazuta Kurauchi. He lived in a Japanese-style house in a lovely section of Fukuoka, on the slopes of the Hirao Reservoir, an area that had escaped the bombing. It was a little piece of old Japan in the midst of the devastation that otherwise constantly assailed our eyes; and in spring the succession of flowering trees and shrubs made it seem like a refuge out of time. One day he invited me to bring some of my buddies for a sukiyaki dinner. One thing bothered us: sukiyaki meant beef, and we knew that beef was particularly scarce and expensive. So we decided to bring along our own, and I so informed Professor Kurauchi. He tried to dissuade us, but we decided to disregard his protestations and we came over lugging a huge mound of beef that we had wangled from our kitchen. Our hosts were nonplussed; bringing the meat had an American brashness about it that was distinctly out of phase with the traditional Japanese etiquette of host–guest relations. But they took it with good grace. The party was extremely pleasant, the food delicious, and the saké abundant.

Mrs. Kurauchi was one of the rare women of that period who had had a higher education, and she was well read and a lively conversationalist. Nevertheless, throughout the entire evening, she acted as the server, not only never once sitting down with us, but in fact sitting on the other side of the *shōji*, the sliding paper doors, in the hallway adjoining the room where we were

sitting, ready to leap up to serve at the slightest sign that the
saké or the food was running low. For a good part of the evening, my two companions simply assumed that she was the
maid. When they realized the situation, they became very embarrassed and tried to cajole her into joining us. Although she
was on the other side of the *shōji* and outside of the room, we
made a point of including her in the conversation, and she frequently did join in. But she remained firmly outside. This was
our first glimpse of traditional Japanese etiquette in a private
setting. We had seen it in restaurants or geisha houses, but
never in a private home and certainly not among highly
educated people.

In general, Japanese people preferred to avoid unpleasant
subjects. Whenever the conversation came around to the war,
you could almost predict how people would behave. First they
would look solemn and sincere, apologize for Japan's miscon-
duct, and shake their heads sadly at the wickedness of the
leaders and the docility of the masses. When it came to more
personal things, like what they had done during the war or how
their families had fared, then there usually came a cheerful
smile, grimly determined not to burden other people with their
own private tragedies. This we could sympathize with. But it
took a long time for us to get used to people saying, "My husband was killed in Rabaul," or "My two sons died in China,"
and then burst out laughing.

The misery that came in the wake of the war was ever-
present whenever we sallied outside our immediate working
and living sphere to see it. Besides those made homeless by the
bombings, approximately seven million Japanese, both military
and civilian, had to be repatriated from the mainland of Asia. A
goodly proportion of these came through the port of Fukuoka,
and they often remained there for days or weeks until they were
able to secure onward transportation. We were always running
across them around the city. It was only much later that I found
out that the sweetheart of Company A, Rikōran, was one of
those repatriates from China who passed through the port of

Fukuoka at the very time that I was there, April 1946. Had I but known . . .

Just as the Japanese were being repatriated from the Asiatic continent, so were Koreans being repatriated to the continent. Korea had been a Japanese colony for thirty-five years, and during this period many Koreans had come to Japan to study or to work. But during the war, when so much Japanese manpower had been drafted into the armed forces, there was a shortage of labor, principally of heavy manual labor—in coal mines, on the wharves, and in heavy construction. Some two million Koreans were brought over to Japan to fill these empty places, taking the heaviest and most menial jobs under conditions approaching impressment, or serfdom. They often lived in barracks, serving under gang bosses, constantly subjected to a military-style discipline, and all for derisory pay. The Fukuoka area was an important center, partly because there were many coal mines around, and partly because Fukuoka was the principal port for repatriation. During the first postwar year, approximately one million Koreans passed through Fukuoka, and while they waited for space on ships they had to be taken care of in transient camps. In this operation the Australian troops played a large role. The Korean repatriation camps became centers of black marketing and crime, and Korean gangs soon became strong enough to challenge already established Japanese gangs, often on their own turf.

On the Korean side there was a strong element of nationalist resentment and the demand that they be accepted as one of the conquerors. The Occupation never quite knew how to deal with them: they were certainly not the enemy, but they were never fully accepted as allies, or as part of the winning team. This, too, was a source of resentment to them; after all, they had been among the very first victims of Japanese imperialism, and yet we still treated them at arm's length. They were given a special status by the Occupation—not enemy, but also not ally; they were "foreign nationals." This entitled them to slightly better treatment than the enemy Japanese (and another class called "enemy nationals," which included Germans and Italians), but not as good as allied nationals.

The Korean camps and squatter settlements sprang up alongside an area that had traditionally been a ghetto for Japan's own untouchables, the so-called *buraku*, or "community," people. Fukuoka was one of the largest untouchable centers in the country. The result of the Koreans moving in on the untouchables was both conflict, as might be expected, and a new fusion of anti-Japanese-majority elements. The untouchables had their own resentments against majority Japanese society, and they often made common cause with Koreans to gain some point or other. Into this explosive situation, which involved hundreds of thousands of people, the intrusion of marines with the blood of combat still in their nostrils, combat veterans anxious to return home, resentful blacks, and Australians only added to the tension.

But none of this was our business. There were others, in the Occupation and the Japanese government, to cope with it, and there was nothing we could do that would make any difference, except to the few people who were the recipients of our gifts of commissary food, cigarettes, or candy.

It was soon plain, however, that even after such a bitter war not everybody was suffering like the repatriates, or the Koreans, or the homeless. The people in Hirao still lived in their gracious houses, and while the official food ration was inadequate and their clothes were getting threadbare, they were able to manage.

The traditional artists and craftsmen were also hard at work despite the struggles of daily life. One I came to know was the Takatori family (also known to connoisseurs as Miraku), one of Japan's most famous pottery dynasties. The Takatori family was a branch of a large pottery clan forcibly brought over from Korea at the end of the sixteenth century. Lord Kuroda of Fukuoka, who had accompanied the invasion forces of the redoubtable Shogun Hideyoshi, was a pottery lover and he, like several other lords, carried off large numbers of Korean pottery establishments, lock, stock, and barrel, to Japan. Many pottery styles today regarded as typically Japanese are in fact Korean, brought over by these Korean immigrants in the sixteenth century.

The incumbent of the Takatori family was the fourteenth generation of his line, and the family specialty was a ceremonial tea bowl. This was my first encounter with Japanese crafts and craftsmen, and it created within me an appetite for pottery, which I never had before, that has lasted me all of my life.

The Takatori establishment was on what was then the western edge of the town leading to the area where many of the great battles with Kublai Khan's Mongol invaders were fought in the thirteenth century. We sometimes went to the vast beaches and tried to imagine the scenes that had once unfolded there: the Mongols over on that side, close to their ships, the Japanese swordsmen on the other side, lurking out from whatever cover of tree, shrub, or sand dune they could find. Then the great wheeling movement of the Mongol horse, the zing of the crossbows, and the thundering hooves of the cavalry rushing at the defenders, the clash of metal, the moiling confusion of horses and men as the horses became useless and then a positive hindrance in the close quarters that left no room for the kinds of maneuvers the Mongols were used to in the vast open spaces of the deserts and steppes of Central Asia, and finally at sundown, both sides retiring to lick their wounds and get ready for the next day's battle. We raced over the trackless beach in our jeep, and once—like a Mongol horse—our jeep wheel fell into a soft spot of sand and we were stalled. We lifted it easily out of its hole and proceeded on our way.

There was on the edge of that particular beach a small hill, or perhaps better, a sand dune, with a shrine of the god Inari at the top. Inari is, among other things, the god of rice and has as his messenger the fox. The distinctive mark of the Inari shrine is the red *torii*, or shrine gates, and the statues of fox messengers. From that beach, dozens of red *torii* curved their way up to the little shrine at the top, flanked by its two fox messengers sitting gravely like sentinels. We climbed up the hill and, as we approached the top, I fancied that I saw a small reddish fox turn to look at us and then run away down the other side of the hill. But then, just the day before I had been reading about foxes and people being possessed by foxes in that part of the country, so I was never quite sure whether I saw a red fox or only a projection of my imagination.

One weekend I took leave to go to the hot-spring resort town of Beppu. The Suginoe Inn, which was then on the waterfront, had been requisitioned as a rest hotel for marine officers. It was a roomy and comfortable old-style inn, quite the opposite of the grand hotel up in the mountains that it has become today. It was run in as close an approximation to Japanese style as the marines could manage: one slept on floor mats, shoes had to be removed, and most of the clientele spent a good part of their time indoors wearing *yukata*, the informal lightweight kimono for sleeping or lounging around. The main concession to American needs was the installation of a cocktail lounge and a small dance floor in the remodeled entranceway.

Each room had its own maid. Mine, let us call Midori. She had that childlike, oval face that always warms the hearts of big, clumsy foreigners and evokes an unexpected paternal desire (even if slightly incestuous) to pat her. Her eyes were tender and often moist, and they looked you straight in the eye as if pleading for support, for an approval that no one could resist giving. Her lips were beautifully formed and framed by a tender chin; she had that tightly formed light-brown skin that is the envy of Nordic sunbathers, which could—and often did—flush to a delicate peach color.

Since I was the only officer at the inn who spoke Japanese—and in fact the first American the maids had ever met who spoke it fluently—I found myself the target of their attention. There were so many things they had always wanted to talk about with the Americans they met, so many words and thoughts that had no outlet. I provided that outlet.

Michiko, a mature woman in her late twenties, who had the

sharp angularity and jutting facial lines of very thin women, had been divorced, and she was a bitter woman. Her husband had tired of her and had "sent her back to her family," as they used to say in old Japan. For a girl to be sent home was a disgrace both to herself and to her family and distinctly lowered her stock on the marriage market. Being tainted, as it were, she was thinking about pulling out of the world of respectable women entirely and going up to the big city as a bar girl, a waitress, or any other of the demimonde occupations that were so easily available. But to do so was no casual matter; it required a willingness to make a decisive break with respectability and with future prospects of marriage. Michiko was on the verge of making this break, and she discussed it often with me. She had reached the point where her only hesitation was not any lingering respectability but rather whether she was pretty enough and whether such prettiness as she had was durable.

Midori, however, was a romantic. And she was in deep trouble. Nineteen years old, with no more than an eighth grade education, she was away from the parental nest for the first time, having had to go to work to support the family. When she left, the family had betrothed her to a policeman in Beppu, and the marriage was scheduled for about six months from that time. Until she went out into the world, this arrangement had satisfied her. She was grateful to her parents for taking the trouble to find her a husband.

But after working for a while with Americans, she was horrified to discover that her view of Japanese men was changing, and she did not like it. "You see," she explained to me, "we have just lost the war. People are poor, they have shabby clothes, they scrabble around to find food. And then, all of a sudden, the Americans come. They are tall, well fed, and have lots of money; their clothes are made of materials we have not seen for years. They are gay, lighthearted, happy. They are attentive to women, they make us feel wanted, they make us feel that it is important to be beautiful. And then we look around at our world: the men are small, shabby, poor; they treat us like servants. It is as if we have suddenly been invaded by an army of Clark Gables." It was flattering to be looked upon as a kind of Clark Gable. Undoubtedly, however, many Japanese men resented this, a resentment that for some took a long time to wash away. It was a commentary both on the depth of Japan's desperation at that time and on the American GIs' infinite capacity to absorb flattery. In any event, life did go on.

And so did the geisha parties and all the other forms of entertainment that smooth the thorny path of social contacts in Japan. High government officials, representatives of the Central Liaison Office (into which the Foreign Office had been transmogrified during the Occupation), and businessmen fell all over themselves to offer entertainment to members of the Occupation. They had a variety of motives: to express friendship; to seduce Americans into liking Japan more; to secure favors; to get to know Americans better; to have an excuse to spend official or corporate funds for a good time. The front runners on the hit parade that season were the American "You Are My Sunshine" and the Japanese "Apple Song":

> Bring your lips to the red apple,
>> The blue sky silently looks on.
> The apple says nothing, but
>> I know how he feels.
> The apple is lovely,
>> Oh, lovely apple.

But the Fukuoka geisha houses had their own favorite, the "Coal Miners Song":

> The moon is out
>> Over the Miike mine.
> The smokestacks so high,
>> The moon is covered with haze.

The fact is that some people did very well. Leave aside the black marketeers: they were a special breed. I remember one evening at a pleasant villa at Lake Yamanaka, near Mount Fuji, a distinguished professor boasting to everyone present about how his family had loaded their godown with cans of food and other supplies to last them through the war. And instead of turning in their gold, silver, and jewels to help the war effort, as all patriotic Japanese had been called on to do, they had hidden them away and were, therefore, now living quite comfortably in spite of the postwar shortages. An appalled look came over the face of a young woman from the provinces as she listened to this. Tears rolled down her cheeks. "Maybe the war was wrong," she said, "maybe we were foolish. But my family contributed all our valuables." Some guests seemed to sympathize with her feelings; others smiled pityingly as if to say, "How stupid of them."

There was a lot to learn. Our training had not prepared us, or at least it had not prepared me, for the reality of Japanese life. I knew little about Japanese society, politics, economy, rural life, literature, or educational system. I knew even less about Japanese psychology, values, social interactions, or ways of thought. If my schooling had not prepared me for these things, neither did my unsystematic reading during our training period.

The BIJs, those who had lived some time in Japan, and those who had studied in universities or in the Army Specialized Training Program had some idea of what to expect. But those, who like me, had had neither personal experience of Japan nor systematic reading and study, did not. I had, of course, rejected the wartime stereotype—the cruel, treacherous, swaggering, fanatic Jap. Not, let me add, through any direct personal knowledge—other than knowing some Japanese-Americans—but because I was an anthropologist and I automatically discounted racial stereotypes.

On the other hand, I had very little to substitute for that other than the images that arose from my reading. And those, as I have already indicated, were largely historical or anthropologically timeless. My image of Japanese men was a cross between the rustic samurai I had read about in Asakawa, the idealistic young samurai who had overthrown the shogunate and established the modernizing Meiji government, and an ultranationalistic military bravo from Japan's famous Kwantung Army. When I first began to associate with actual Japanese people, I was surprised not to find these types lurking behind closed *shōji* doors in the next room, or in the corridors outside the room.

Farmers, for example, came to me as a great revelation. My first encounter with one was near the city of Dazaifu. Dazaifu had been the ancient capital of Kyushu, or the Western Circuit, as it was known in the seventh and eighth centuries. But even after that, perhaps because it was the home of the great shrine of Hachiman, the god of war, it retained an aura of secret power, even of holiness. Dazaifu was about twenty miles from Fukuoka City. Several of us had lost our way back to Fukuoka and stopped the jeep to ask directions of a group of farmers along the roadside. The scene was one of bucolic peace and prosperity. If not for the Japanese faces, it might have been one of those rollicking peasant scenes that Rubens used to paint. There were old ladies carrying bundles of twigs on their backs, sturdy housewives with produce in basketry backpacks, men carrying hoes or scythes, a horse drawing a small wagon, and among this randomly gathered group there was the kind of intimate laughing and joking that comes from many generations of close relations and an absence of worry about what tomorrow might bring. Or, at least, that is the way it looked to me after the depressing sights of inner Fukuoka. When we put our question to one of the farmers, he led us to a clearing at the side of the road. He then picked up a twig and, on the firm packed soil, he drew us a map. It would have done credit to a professional cartographer. When he realized that we spoke Japanese, he became less formal and chatted with us. How did we like Dazaifu? Then he recited a poem for us. I was so intrigued—and also because my Japanese was not up to the demands of poetry and his local accent—that I asked him to write it out. He did so, and later on I showed it to a friend at the university. It went:

137

Splendid is the moon,
   and crystalline sounds the river's purl.
Come, let us all revel,
   we who go to the capital
   and we who stay behind.*

I must confess I was startled to learn that it was not just some local Chamber of Commerce plug for the old hometown but from the *Manyōshū*, the great eighth-century compilation of poetry.

Why I should have been so surprised I am not sure. I suppose that we had some fixed image in our minds of "the Asian peasant" as an unlettered, downtrodden serf, and to have one act out of character was a shock. Later on, when I was doing studies in preparation for the Occupation's land reform program, I often had occasion to remember that incident when I would run into still another example of the very high cultural level that one encounters in Japanese villages. Before starting my Latin American career I had spent a good period of time doing rural sociological studies in southern Illinois. Nothing in my experience had prepared me for the sight of a farmer reciting ancient poetry.

The customs, the forms of interaction, and the ways of living were not the issue. For these could not be taught; they could only be described. One had to experience them personally for a period of time in order to absorb them. Therefore, while I was stationed in Fukuoka, although my job was censoring telecommunications, my true vocation, if such I can call it, was to penetrate as deeply as I could into Japanese thought and culture, to get inside its skin, so to speak. My encounter with Japan was essentially the unfolding of that pursuit. To that end, I made a point of meeting all kinds of people—professors,

*Poem No. 571, from the *Manyōshū* (*The Ten Thousand Leaves*), a collection of earlier poetry compiled in the eighth century. Ian Hideo Levy, *The Ten Thousand Leaves*, Princeton: Princeton University Press, 1981, vol. 1, p. 276.

gangsters, government officials, geisha house madams, students, innkeepers. I walked the streets, I tried everything that came my way, I read newspapers and books, and I constantly searched out new experiences. That is, I used the techniques that anthropologists call "participant observation." For this kind of knowledge, personal experience was better than books.

Our main problem in understanding Japanese life was to balance the contradictory generalizations, each of which seemed to be applicable, even if to different people or to the same people at different times. It was this that Ruth Benedict had tried to explicate in her image of the chrysanthemum and the sword. Each of these images was correct; each represented one side of the Japanese character. The problem was to understand the deep grounding within which they were united. Our expectation was that Japanese women would be modest in demeanor, if not as extreme as the *Yamato-nadeshiko*—literally "the wild pink (a flower) of Yamato" (the old name for Japan), that is, a beautiful woman of typical, classic Japanese type—then certainly closer to that pole than to the opposite extreme. And, to be sure, Japanese women were modest, retiring, gracious.

But at the same time there was an entirely different image of Japanese women that came from the experience foreigners had had with prostitutes and geisha, from the occasional literature that had been translated into English, and from the concept held by some foreign observers that the Japanese did not have the puritanical hang-ups of Americans. How could that image of modesty be reconciled with the street girls (the *panpan*, a postwar phenomenon), the houses of prostitution, the *mama-san*, or madams of bars, teahouses, restaurants, inns, and geisha houses? And even away from the demimonde of professional women catering to the needs of men (called *mizu-shōbai*, or the "water trades"), how could the image of modesty and demureness be reconciled with the raucous women in fishing villages, or with the hardheaded business women in Tokyo's "downtown" or in Osaka's merchant districts? In my first summer in Japan, hot and steaming, I had seen country women

139

walking around bare-breasted outside their houses. And I can remember my sense of shock when I first encountered mixed bathing in bathhouses and hot-spring resorts.

It is not surprising that many Americans thought they had come to some paradise where the attitude toward sex was straightforward and unpuritanical. Later on, Japanese began to become much more self-conscious about these matters, partly, one suspects, in fear of being looked down upon by foreigners as barbarians. But our problem was how to reconcile these conflicting images of Japanese women. Was it simply that some Japanese were one way, others another way? Or did the Japanese have the same range of heterogeneity as other societies; was this just the surface presented to outsiders; could the same person vary depending upon circumstances?

The family, we were told, was very important. Yet we saw men who devoted themselves so completely to their work that they virtually spent no time with their families. And when they met others or entertained, it was always outside the home. To an American this was hard to understand. If you said of an American that he was a "family man," you expected that he would spend as much time with his family as he could, that he would meet people and entertain not in public places but at home, and that he would involve his family—if not the children, at least his wife—in his social affairs. But to go to a Japanese home and spend the evening with the husband alone, the wife acting only as a servant to deliver the food and the drink, was somehow not consistent with our image of the "family man."

We had also learned through our casual readings that Japan was a country of piety and protocol. The shrines and temples were always milling with people and the festivals were gay, but most people seemed totally disinterested in religion. Coming from a land where Sunday church-going was a major institution, the casualness about religion we saw everywhere did not square with our definition of religiosity. My image of the austerity of the Zen priest was also shattered by the first one I came to know as a personal friend. He was earthy, a sturdy drinker, and a womanizer, and he described himself as a *namagusa-bozu*, a "fresh-grass monk," that is, a monk still not freed from the lusts of the flesh. I was used to clerics who were pious.

One of our greatest problems was learning how to read the signals that we received from our Japanese friends and associates. Americans, for example, were easily flattered by the signs of deference they received from Japanese, even from high-placed ones. The natural human tendency was to believe that people sincerely meant all the laudatory things they were saying and to take the words at face value. But when they realized that much of this was formal politeness, etiquette, and protocol, the tendency was to go to the opposite extreme and accuse the Japanese of dishonesty and insincerity. Americans were always having difficulty reconciling these two reactions because they were unable to comprehend the protocol of superordinate–subordinate relations and of host–guest relations in Japan.

It is very common in Japan, partly as a mark of respect or deference, for a person to call upon a guest or a superior for advice. "Maestro, please teach me," is a common formula. Usually the speaker does not mean literally that he wishes to receive education or instruction in the particular matter at issue, but since the protocol is so different from the corresponding American one under the circumstances, many Americans misunderstood and felt that they were literally being called upon to teach. All too many were quite willing to comply. And so there were many comical scenes of Americans complying with alacrity to please, and the Japanese having to sit through another tedious sermon they were too polite to cut off.

During those early postwar days, many personal and family tragedies were still very fresh in people's minds. Americans expect that when people refer to their tragedies, their manner will be somber and sad. That Japanese would mention their tragedies and immediately break out into what appeared to be hilarious laughter came as a shock. It was hard for those without experience of Japan in those days to realize the complex psychological factors that went into that kind of laughter: the desire to avoid imposing one's problems on the listener; the desire to avoid the implication that the American (usually in the military) might have been responsible for the tragedy; the desire to steer the situation away from sadness toward normality. But to many Americans such behavior seemed to show a lack of human feeling.

In other words, we often had difficulty reading the signals that were being conveyed to us. Sometimes we expected the Japanese to behave like Americans, and when they did not we tended to think there was something wrong with them. Sometimes, to the contrary, we expected them to be totally different, and when they were not, we were equally surprised. We were always getting the signs wrong.

I also had to learn the basic elements of my job. When I was in Fukuoka censoring telecommunications, this was not much of a task. But when, after three months, I was transferred to Tokyo to take charge of public opinion and sociological research, I began to feel the shortcomings of our preparation very keenly.

In the public opinion field, for example, I had to work a great deal with the Prime Minister's Office. But I had not the foggiest idea of its role, where it fit into the organizational structure of government, and what its powers and jurisdictions were. I also had responsibility for putting a bill through the Diet, Japan's parliament. But I had not the slightest idea of how the Diet worked, its composition, its committee structure, the legislative process. All of these I had to learn about pragmatically because we had done no preparatory study in the language school. It was a good two years, for example, before I realized that Japan's single-entry, multimember electoral constituency system was unique.

Perhaps it did not matter, one might say. After all, the Occupation had for a period of time virtually supreme authority,

and to get something done we did not need to know, we had only to command. Whether I understood the Cabinet Bureau or
not, whether I understood the structure of the Diet or not, it
was up to my counterparts in the Japanese government to see
to it that my bill went through. That was, in a sense, true, and it
was the position taken by many American Occupation officials.
They also did not think it was necessary for us to know the
Japanese language. But I did.

Soon after I was assigned to Tokyo, my unit became involved
in some studies related to the Occupation's land reform program. This program was one of the greatest achievements of
the Occupation, although, alas, very few Americans seem to
know about it or to care. Within approximately a two-year
period, it put an end to landlordism in Japan, and it accomplished this without bloodshed or revolution. The contribution of
the land reform to Japan's postwar development cannot be
overestimated. In any event, when I started on this research, I
drew upon my rural sociological research in southern Illinois
during my graduate student days, my knowledge of black
sharecroppers in the American South, my experience with
Mexican peasants, and my general reading in the fields of anthropology and rural sociology. But I was wrong. I did not even
have a vocabulary to describe the new phenomena that came to
my attention. The *oyakata–kokata* relation, for example. I knew
about patron–client relations as a theoretical issue in anthropology, and I knew the *caciques* and *peones* and the
caudillismo of Mexico. I was also aware that slavery-derived
sharecropping or tenant farming in many parts of the old South
involved clientelistic elements. But none of this prepared me
for the *oyakata–kokata* systems I saw in many parts of Japan.
Fortunately, I had good teachers. I had as advisors some of
Japan's leading rural sociologists, and I also benefited from
association with the great folklorist Kunio Yanagita and his
disciples and coworkers.

This was the position of many of my fellow language students
who were assigned to substantive Occupation posts. Except for

the handful with prior knowledge and experience, or those with specialized knowledge, it was a case of on-the-job training.

VI *

A TOWN
IN THE NORTH

The on-the-job training was a kind of shock treatment, but it was pleasant shock. Between 1946 and 1948, my unit did surveys in about thirty villages all over Japan, some for the Occupation's land reform, some for the fishery reform. I personally took part in at least half of the field trips. Each brought me deeper into Japan. What I observed began to blend with what I had been reading and with my personal experiences, and all of it started to take on new shapes and significance.

The Hairy Ainu

In December 1947, I went with one of our research teams to Daté-Monbetsu, on the south coast of the northern island of Hokkaido. (At that time, Daté-Monbetsu was only a town; in the 1960s it became legally a city.) It was one of the sample points we had selected for our study of fishery rights; but for me it had a special appeal because I knew that it contained a large Ainu community. The "hairy Ainu," it will be recalled, are the survivors of the aboriginal inhabitants of the Japanese islands. To the anthropologist they are an intriguing problem because, while culturally they show many affinities with the so-called circumpolar peoples—the Eskimos, the Chukchi of the Siberian tundras, the Gilyak—physically they are different both from them and from their neighbors, the Japanese. They seem to represent some earlier Caucasoid strain that has either disappeared in other parts of the world or been so completely absorbed that it is no longer recognizable as a distinct entity. Heavy body hair, brown hair ranging from light to dark, occasional greenish eyes, and no epicanthic (Mongoloid) fold all distinguish them from the Japanese and the other neighboring Mongoloid peoples.

When the ancient Japanese first arrived, they found the Ainu all over the main islands. Because they were hunters, fishermen, and gatherers, the Ainu never attained the large populations of settled farming communities. Of all the aboriginal groups the Japanese encountered, it was the Ainu who, in the end, gave the most trouble and took the longest time to subdue. As the Yamato coalition of tribes and clans, which eventually formed the Japanese nation, made its way slowly northward from its original home farther south, it fought the Ainu all along. Local chieftains who declared their vassalage to the Japanese were often left in place and even, in some cases, absorbed into the Japanese nobility; those who resisted were wiped out or driven off. Step by step the Ainu were driven to the north, finally ending up on the bleak, uninhabited northern island of Hokkaido, where virtually all of them are concentrated today.

The wars against the Ainu form a part of the romantic history of Japan, much like our own westward expansion against the Indians. The principal difference is that our experience is a recent one, while the Japanese experience took place more slowly, over a longer period of time, and has receded into the mists of ancient history. Nevertheless, the Ainu wars bred their own heroes, legends, and folk types. The northeast marches, on the frontier of settlement, were guarded by a tough breed of men, the *Azuma-bito*, the "men out of the East." Coarse and virile, their visits to the Imperial capital of Kyoto stirred the same

146

mixed thrill among the refined, well-bred, gentle, and civilized that frontiersmen and barbarians have always done throughout history. *Azuma otoko, Kyō onna*, the old proverb goes, "an Eastern man and a Kyoto woman." This is the proverbial prescription for the perfect combination—the tough virility of the frontiersman, the refinement and delicacy of the civilized woman.

Even the office of shogun owes something to the Ainu wars. *Shōgun*, which means "great general," or "generalissimo," is an abbreviation of the larger title, *Sei-i-tai-shōgun*, or "barbarian-subduing generalissimo." This title was first given in 794, to the commander of the forces sent to subdue the Ainu in the east. Although the title was in principle a temporary commission granted by the Imperial Court, once the military rule was established, it became hereditary *de facto*, used by the leader of the military classes.

In the course of time, virtually all of the Ainu were wiped out, absorbed into the mainstream Japanese stock through intermarriage, or driven to the northern island of Hokkaido. In 1947 there were somewhat over twenty thousand, today rather less, most of them of mixed Ainu-Japanese parentage. Pure-blood Ainu of the classical type number no more than two thousand. For several centuries they were protected by their remoteness, since Hokkaido was not the Japanese idea of a pleasant place to live. But with the end of the nineteenth century, when the Japanese began to settle Hokkaido seriously as a matter of national policy, the Ainu found themselves reduced to second-class citizenship in their last refuge.

This time, they were not physically exterminated, as in the earlier period, although the Japanese settlers brought with them a traditional racial contempt. According to one folk etymology, the name Ainu is derived from the Japanese words *a inu*, or roughly, "Ah! a dog." The etymology is undoubtedly mistaken, but it expresses deeply rooted attitudes. With the colonization of Hokkaido, what usually happened was that the small Ainu communities were left in place but surrounded by

147

growing Japanese populations. Hunters and fishermen, they innocently allowed the Japanese settlers to take over the arable lands for cultivation, and they themselves were quickly reduced to the status of a landless, poverty-stricken lower class. In the Daté-Monbetsu area, for example, the only settlement had been the small Ainu hamlet of Usu. When the Japanese immigrants first began to arrive in 1869 from the great northern feudal domain of Sendai, they settled all around the Ainu. Usu Hamlet was incorporated administratively, along with seven other hamlets, into the township of Daté-Monbetsu.

Hokkaido

Hokkaido, the "northern sea road," was the last of the four main islands to be settled by the Japanese. Yezo, as it used to be called, was not the kind of place the Japanese liked to live. It was too cold and it was not good for growing rice. The principal inhabitants were a few Gilyak (tribesmen related to the tundra peoples of Siberia), Ainu, soldiers, and fishermen. In 1604, the island was assigned over to the Matsumae feudal domain, which established a modest capital city today called Fukuyama. Its port city was Hakodaté.

Over the centuries Buddhist temples had carried on a modest, intermittent evangelical effort to civilize the aborigines, and garrisons had been established at strategic spots. Daté-Monbetsu's principal temple, Zenkōji, for example, claims a very long history. There is an old tradition that it was established by the great monk Kuya from the Mount Hiei monastery near Kyoto in the tenth century. Kuya—who was one of the founders of the popular sect of Pure Land Buddhism (as against the traditional Esoteric Buddhism that was virtually limited to the Imperial Court)—went as an evangelist to the Ainu to show that Buddhism was for everybody and that not even the humblest were to be excluded from Paradise. The present temple is dated from the end of the sixteenth century. Unfortunately most of the records were destroyed by fire.

That there was a vigorous religious center in the sixteenth

and seventeenth centuries, however, cannot be doubted. One of the temple's treasures is a small stone lantern dated 1639, with the curious figure known as Maria-Kwannon carved on its face. At first sight, it appears to be the Buddhist goddess of mercy, Kwannon; but on closer look, one can see that it is a carefully disguised image of the Virgin Mary. These statues are relics of the persecution of Christianity in Japan in the seventeenth century. After the so-called Shimabara Rebellion of Christian peasants had been put down in the southern island of Kyushu in 1638, Christianity virtually disappeared from Japan, continuing only in remote rural districts, or in forms designed to deceive the authorities. Some of these figurines are called "Oribé lanterns," because of the belief that the great seventeenth-century Kyoto tea master, Oribé Furuta, was a secret Christian. Esoteric belief has it that Oribé planted these Maria-Kwannon lanterns around the garden of his tea ceremony house. This pathetic reminder of the persecutions of Christians suggests that some secret Christian may have run off to the wilds of Yezo, or that there may even have been some secret Christians among the Buddhist missionaries.

But despite these scattered and intermittent efforts, it was not until the end of the eighteenth century, when the Russians began to make their ominous appearance around the Sea of Okhotsk, that the Japanese government started to take Yezo seriously. The Russian presence had in fact been building up for at least a century. Their own "manifest destiny" had already led them across Siberia by the seventeenth century. In 1649 they established a base on the Sea of Okhotsk and from there probed Kamchatka and the surrounding seas. In the early eighteenth century, tendrils moved down into Sakhalin, the Kuriles, and finally to the island of Hokkaido itself. These moves, Americans will recall from our own history, were related to the Russian explorations and settlements in Alaska, Northern California, and the Hawaiian islands.

Although in the end it was the American, Commodore Matthew Calbraith Perry, who finally broke open the doors of

Japan's isolation, it is salutary to remember that the Russians had been at work on this for some time. Perry and his black ships arrived in Japan in July 1853; but Russian Admiral Putiatin dropped anchor in Nagasaki harbor in August, only one month later.

The Founding of Daté

The town of Daté-Monbetsu has an honorable place in this curious history. When the shoguns became alarmed about the Russians, they ordered the feudal domains nearest Yezo to become more active there. But since this order benefited from neither the carrot nor the stick, most of the feudal lords dawdled along, unwilling to spend their own resources for the heavy cost of garrisoning troops, building defense works, land reclamation, and settlement. The main exception was the Nambu feudal domain (corresponding to the present Iwate Prefecture in the north of the main island), which did make some energetic moves, including strengthening its fisheries operations in the bleak northern island. For the tough Nambu men, Hokkaido was probably not so difficult. Their own home, which used to be described as the "Tibet of Japan," was in the rugged mountains of the northern part of the main island, where the winters are as severe as, if not even more severe than, in Yezo. (The climate of southern Yezo is milder than Nambu's.) Many of the men remained away from home in fisheries or garrison duty for long periods, and as is the way with single men in remote lands, they began to take Ainu women as wives or mistresses. It is from this practice that came the proverb, *Nambu otoko ni me no ko,* "a Nambu man and an Ainu woman."

The Daté Domain, ruled by the lords of Sendai, was the largest and most powerful of the northern domains. During the battles of the Meiji Restoration in 1868, it made the mistake of siding with the losers, so partly in punishment and partly because of its resources, the young Meiji government ordered it to take on the colonization of southern Hokkaido. The order was received in 1869. It was simple. According to the scroll,

150

then in the possession of the Daté family: "You are ordered to take control of the district of Usu." By March 1870, the first party of two hundred and fifty men from Daté, most of them samurai, arrived in the region known to the Ainu as Monbetsu, or Eburi, "the red land," and immediately set about the reclamation of land for farming. The small pioneer community was in the charge of a cadet branch of the House of Daté, and the early pioneering activities were carried out under the strict discipline of the traditional lord–vassal relationship. It was not until 1879, when a village office came to be established, that Daté-Monbetsu shifted to a modern system of public authority.

Daté never became the great center it was intended to be. Instead, it ended up as a modest farming and fishing village. The samurai pioneers imperceptibly, but rapidly, turned into good farmers, fishermen, storekeepers, and officials. Because as samurai they placed great value on education, Daté became, in 1872, the first village in Hokkaido to start a modern elementary school. Daté is still aware of its unique social background, commemorated by the cherry blossom motif in the official town crest.*

The settlement of Hokkaido was urgently necessary, in the view of the young Meiji reformers, to build up Hokkaido's population, resources, and defenses, if they were to forestall any move by the Russians and strengthen their own *de jure* title. But Hokkaido presented much the same kind of problem to the Japanese as Alaska to the United States. It was remote, and the styles of living that had laboriously developed through the

*"The cherry blossom symbolizes the chivalric spirit of the samurai pioneers, the first settlers of the town. The river is the symbol of our geographical location: our area abounds in pure rivers. The term *betsu*, which appears in the ancient names of Monbetsu or Osarubetsu, is the Ainu word for 'pure river.' The circle represents harmony: the early settlers overcame the classical 'thousand trials and ten thousand tribulations' only through mutual love and the sharing of hardship between lord and vassal." (Translated from the *Outline of Daté*, the official town history, dated 1961.)

centuries of life in milder climates could not be used there. Rice was almost impossible to grow; Japanese houses could not stand up to the bitter northern winters. New tools, techniques, architecture, methods of cultivation, crops, food habits, clothing, and ways of life would have to be developed before the north country could become home.

For help in conquering this new environment, the Japanese turned to the more developed northern countries, the United States, Switzerland, Sweden, and Russia. Among the foreign advisors, Americans were far and away in the majority, and the American mark on the Hokkaido landscape is still noticeable. Hokkaido University itself is a monument to American advisors, having started out as close to the model of a land-grant college as was possible in Japan of the day. Its agricultural department was organized by William Smith Clark, a specialist from the Massachusetts Agricultural College (today, the University of Massachusetts), who gave Meiji Japan one of its most memorable slogans in his farewell speech to the Sapporo College of Agriculture: "Boys, be ambitious!" One comes on oddly familiar landscapes, hip-roofed barns and silos like Wisconsin's, placid herds of cattle grazing in vast pastures, church steeples rising from the midst of small settlements reminiscent of pioneer Midwestern towns.

Hot-Spring Interlude

My party arrived in Daté-Monbetsu in the rapidly thinning light of a late December afternoon. We had just completed a rugged two weeks in the cold northwest coast of Hokkaido, where we had been virtually snowbound all the time. It was so cold there on the drafty floors, in spite of wood-burning stoves and heated floor pits, that I had to sleep in my parka, with the hood over my head. Aside from the single-track rail line, which could not always be relied on when the blizzards were blowing and the snow piled high on the tracks, our main mode of transportation had been horse sled. En route to Daté-Monbetsu, we managed one night in the hot springs of Noboribetsu. The Noboribetsu

Dai-Ichi Hotel was, at that time, probably the largest hot-spring hotel in all of Japan. On first glance a rambling frame structure, it was in reality a series of Japanese buildings strung together by long corridors and patchwork roofing that stretched up the hills from its placid valley toward the permanent hot-spring geysers bubbling up from underground. The Japanese call these geysers "hell springs." The hotel sheltered over thirty different hot-spring pools, each having a different kind of water: some hot, some cold, some containing radium, or sulphur, or phosphorus.

When our bodies, still rigid from the cold of the Arctic Mashike coast, first touched those healing waters, a kind of delirium took hold. We staggered from pool to pool; when we were about to faint from the near-boiling sulphur springs, we flopped into a sobering pool of cold water, and so on, from one to the next. One member of our party claimed to have tried all thirty of the pools, although none of us was in a proper condition to confirm or disconfirm his boast. After one was completely exhausted from the hot baths, one's heart would begin to beat dangerously fast, and the deep lassitude would lead one to dally pleasantly with fantasies of death as little more than an agreeable fading away into these endless pools. This was the time to get out.

Even the endless unheated corridors one had to traverse back to one's room could not extinguish the warming heat stored so deeply in all the cells of the body. The technique was to recover from one bath through massages, saké, and food, and then go back again and again, until finally one returned to the room and fell asleep. During the big party of some seventy people that the prefectural authorities threw for us, I myself went back about five times. *Only* five times, I should say, because my Japanese colleagues, who could stand the hot baths better than I, went far more often. "Don't you like the baths?" someone asked me when once I refused still another sortie.

The baths were a spectacular scene, especially with a little saké fuzzing the edge of one's vision. It was like entering a hillside of geysers, with jets of steam rising all around and steam clouds making it impossible to see more than a few feet ahead. Vague shapes loomed and faded in the mid-distance, and for all that there must have been several hundred people—men, women, and children—in the baths, one had a sense of ineffable privacy. Tender little vignettes formed and unformed: a young mother in a trance of bliss, eyes focused somewhere beyond the clouds of steam, languidly scrubbing her seven-year-old daughter, who sighed ecstatically whenever some especially delicious spot was touched; two lovers shut within their own refulgence, turned slightly away from each other but grimly pressed naked back to naked back; an efficient geisha trying to handle her beamingly drunk client, an elderly gentleman obviously of some stature, trying first to go to sleep on the tile floors and then quite happily letting his limp body sink under water—she propped him upright, carefully scrubbed him all over, rinsed him with buckets of hot water, and then held him carefully to prevent him from sinking completely out of sight; an elderly grandmother sighing blissfully as she surrendered her body to the hot water, her flat dugs floating lightly on the surface; a young geisha leading a still sober young client by the hand as they searched for a private spot—later I saw them holding hands, she on the edge of the pool dangling her feet and he in the water, as the sparks flew almost visibly back and forth between them; young boys racing each other on the slippery tile floors, sliding and skidding into the cold pools.

The Town Hall

The next morning, thoroughly purged, we drove the forty or so miles to Daté-Monbetsu in a fleet of prewar vintage cars. Our party—which consisted of myself as team leader and about ten Japanese anthropologists, rural sociologists, fishery experts, economists, and cartographers—was hustled into the town office. The paint on the rambling wooden structure was so ancient it was scarcely visible; where it did show through, it was peeling and cracked. We walked through corridors down which the wind whistled, and were finally led into a formal meeting room where I noticed gratefully that an old-fashioned, pot-bellied Hokkaido stove was showing red on its rounded cheeks. With that unerring instinct the Japanese have for protocol, the crowd of fifty or so men sorted itself out rapidly, and we found ourselves seated around a rectangle of four tables with a hollow center, everyone in his proper place. The senior Japanese scholars with me and the village leaders were casually disposed in the more honored locations; the graduate students and junior faculty members had automatically moved to the lower positions. The mayor, the head of the fishery cooperative, the head of the agricultural cooperative, and the liaison officer from the prefectural government surrounded me at the leading table, their aides disposing themselves in order of rank and age among the rest of my party.

The tables were covered by long green felt pads, scraped up especially for the occasion, and at each place a small sweet, wrapped in paper, had been placed. This, as is the custom in Japan, is to be taken with the hot, bitter tea. It is made of that special Japanese red bean, the *azuki*, that forms the base of almost all traditional Japanese sweets. Balanced by the bitter tea, it makes an interesting taste; by itself, it is too sweet for the Western palate. The decorative teen-age girls, who filed in to pour our tea and then stood around respectfully waiting to refill any emptied cups, were clerks in the town office. As was the custom, they also served as maids, waitresses, and cup bearers when the need arose.

Many of the men in the room were unusually large for Japanese, their barrel chests straining at the unfamiliar Western-style jackets they had put on for the occasion. One in particular had the broad face and powerful bone structure of the professional *sumo* wrestler. His jacket was so tight that his arms could not rest normally at his sides or in his lap; instead, the pull from the armholes and the barrelling of his chest shoved the upper arms out and, from his slightly forward-bent elbows, his forearms dangled uncertainly. He had the friendly, almost puppyish look of the outsize man who had never been able to come to terms with his own size. He is always knocking over vases and bumping into people with an apologetic expression that seems to say, "I can't think what this huge body is doing on little old me."

The oversized in Japan have even more difficulty than seven footers in the United States. All of the standard proportions of the traditional Japanese house and way of life are designed for shorter people. They bump their heads on doorways when they enter rooms, their feet stick out of the bed covers at night, theater seats are too narrow for them, economy-class airplane seats won't hold their bulk, stores do not stock their size in sandals. During the war, the army had to defer *sumo* wrestlers and other big men because they were just too much trouble to handle. *Sumo* wrestlers were allocated special rations because they would starve on the rations of ordinary people. Nowadays, even though the Japanese are getting taller and heavier, one has the impression that people are so conditioned to the notion that they are small that it is a surprise to them that their bodies are so large. In any gathering you will find these new outsized Japanese teetering on legs too long for them, ready to topple over as if they were made of building blocks piled up just off center; they bend from the waist to get closer to a size they feel more comfortable with. The embarrassed giant at the meeting, it turned out, was one of the leading officials of the fishery cooperative. Later, at parties, I found him a drinker on the same scale as his physical size, always ready to belt out a solo or to lead a group of fishermen in their chants and sea ditties.

We sat in our overcoats through the formal speeches of welcome, the explanations of our mission, and the offers of cooperation. The pot-bellied stove warmed up its spot of the room, but it was not strong enough to counterbalance the draft pouring in from the corridor. When we had had our last sip of tea and finished all the necessary bows, we set off for our inn.

The Hamlet of Usu

The Kawara was a standard Japanese-style inn with a few crude frontier touches—pot-bellied stove instead of the traditional charcoal brazier, heavy drapes against the sliding doors to keep out the air, locally made rough-hewn deal tables. We looked out on the glassy smooth waters of Usu Bay, which was formed by an inlet from the sea broadened into a round basin. Black-green shadows of cliffs, like a Japanese ink drawing, showed on the left. Glass floats were strung out like bubbles on the surface. A lonely gull cried out like a baby. An elderly Ainu out for some early evening shellfish worked his gear with practiced hand in a long, flat-bottomed boat, occasionally reaching back to warm his hands on the brazier in the stern. Usu was the heart of the Ainu community.

After dinner we went out to pay a call on Yaeko. Yaeko was an Ainu woman who had been adopted as a young girl by the famous missionary, John Bachelor, and raised as a proper Christian in their Sapporo home. Bachelor, who is known primarily for his pioneering work on the Ainu, had come to Hokkaido in 1877, lived there for some sixty years, and then died in Canada on home leave during World War II. Because of him, a good proportion of the Ainu had been converted to Christianity. Wherever he went, he built small churches in Ainu communities, so that in some parts of Hokkaido one saw churches and steeples that seemed oddly out of place in a Japanese village. Usu had been his favorite place, and here he built a house. The seedy little hamlet boasted a noble stone church, built under Bachelor's inspiration in 1886, which looked like a small version of a European cathedral sitting on its hilltop overlooking the homes of the faithful below.

When the Bachelors could not return to wartime Japan, Yaeko gave up the Sapporo house and moved back to Usu. There, she spent her time taking care of the Bachelor property and acting as caretaker of the church. "Nowadays," she said sadly, "it is hardly used except on Christmas or Easter."

Having only known her from the photographs in one of Bachelor's books captioned "Yaeko as a young girl," and "Yaeko as a young woman," I was not prepared for the sixty-year-old woman who met us. She was short, dressed in generically Western clothes, although apparently in many layers of them. Intense and darkly handsome, she had the characteristic Ainu features—large, round, light-green eyes, without the Mongoloid fold, smooth, rounded face, light olive skin. Her graying dark hair was drawn back in a loose bun. Her shoulders were slightly bent, not with age but rather with the intensity of the exhorter, the organizer. There was a practiced sulkiness about her, as if permanent grievance had become part of herself. She immediately folded you into her private conspiracy and spoke in disconnected fragments as if you knew what she was talking about.

The Bachelors, it seems, had adopted her not with the intention of saving her from her people but rather of making her a model of what a modern, educated, Christian Ainu could be. She had been educated both in Japanese and English, learned to behave as a proper Japanese woman as well as a Christian, but she also had to learn to speak Ainu properly. All around her, the Ainu were losing their language and culture and becoming impoverished, low-class Japanese. Like Bachelor, she saw Christianity as the only hope of preserving Ainu cultural values in the modern world. She was so deeply a part of Bachelor's mission that she had never had time to marry.

"But these people have no pride in their ancestry," she said. "Now that Bachelor-*sensei* is no longer around, they don't even go to church any more. And some of them still call themselves Christians!"

"Have they become Buddhists?" I asked. "They're too lazy even to become Buddhists," she told me scornfully. "They just drift along with no thought for the future. And I'm not talking just about the eternal future. They don't even think about their own immediate future right here in Usu."

Her story was not a new one. The Ainu have always been used as a textbook example of the population decline that often sets in among "primitive" peoples on contact with modern civilization. Nothing dramatic seems to happen; they continue

158

smiling, but they sicken and die. How the biology of this works it would be hard to say, but there is no doubt that seemingly healthy people simply stop producing children. It is as if they have lost the will to survive as a separate entity, and this collective death-wish is manifested through sterility. There does not seem to have been any of this before the late nineteenth century. But since that time, the Ainu population has declined drastically, and most of them are mixed Japanese-Ainu or even pure ethnic Japanese. Ainu families without children often adopted orphaned Japanese children to raise as their own, so that many of those called Ainu are really ethnic Japanese who have been raised by Ainu families and think of themselves as Ainu.

The malaise goes so deep that younger people were at that time ashamed of being Ainu and, like many of our own immigrant groups, were desperate to be accepted as Japanese. To achieve this, they would unlearn their Ainu, despise the "absurd customs of the past," learn Japanese in the schools, and, if possible, marry Japanese rather than Ainu.

"Did you see any old women on the street on your way over here?" one of the old men visiting Yaeko asked me.

I recalled that I did not. "That's because the young people hide them away when strangers come around. They don't want anyone to see their tattoos. Those old ladies have to be shut away in dark corners of the house as if they were lepers, or foul monsters to be ashamed of. Their own mothers, mind you."

The traditional Ainu tattooing was indeed something to behold. Part of their reputation for hairiness came, of course, from their genuine hirsuteness, their beards, moustaches, hairy chests, and shocks of bushy hair, but part also came from their elaborate tattooing, which made them look hairy, whether they were or not. The old ladies, in particular, were spectacular examples of the needleman's art: blue-black on the upper lip to look like flowing moustaches; wrinkles tattooed on the forehead; rings on wrist and arms that were artfully made to look like bracelets and armlets. I found that with some of the older ladies the tattooing had faded so that it could only be detected in good light. Under the age of fifty, there are practically no tattooed people, I was told.

Usu Hamlet was perhaps more sensitive about this issue than most. Bachelor had tried to instill in them that most impossible of combinations: respect for their traditional culture along with Christianity, education, and modern aspirations. Although these might be held together in tenuous solution by rare personalities, in ordinary life as it confronts these disappearing people, the solution is not viable.

The Usu people, for example, refused in an exemplary fashion to turn themselves into tourist curiosities as did some Ainu groups in other towns. There the tourist Ainu would put on a complete show for you, even a "ceremonial" bear feast, if you wished. They live on the Japanese tourists' thirst for the exotic and supply it at fixed rates just as do some of our own American Indians. They flaunt their full-flowing beards to give the Japanese the thrill of having seen a real "hairy Ainu," wear the traditional linen kimono, perform ceremonies in the open or in traditional Ainu houses, serve Ainu food, sell "Ainu crafts" (perhaps made in a Japanese factory), such as wood carvings of bears holding salmon in their mouths.

The Usu Ainu bent over so far backward that they would not wear Ainu clothing or draw attention to themselves as Ainu in any way. My first reaction to all this was admiration for old man Bachelor for having given them enough inner pride in being Ainu to refuse to make an exhibition of themselves. But no sooner did I formulate my admiration for this exemplary attitude when I realized it was not as simple as that. They refused to be tourist Ainu not only because they were too proud to do so but also because they were ashamed of being Ainu at all.

"So I suppose there's no chance of hearing any old Ainu music or dancing," I speculated aloud. There was a sudden pause. The two old men present looked at each other, smiled, and then said, "Sure, we'll be glad to show them to you." I thereupon invited them to my inn for a party the next night.

"And bring some friends. I'd like to hear about Ainu life in the old days," I said.

An Ainu Party

The next night, the two old men showed up at the inn with five friends, three old men and two old women. "We're all old people," they apologized. "Young people don't know the old dances." With my research team and entourage, we numbered about twenty-five people, and so the inn opened the special party room for us on the second floor, which they made up by removing the sliding door partitions between two large rooms. The maids moved around the large party room pouring the saké, and soon our guests began to relax.

"You won't believe it," one of the old men said, "but I am probably the only Ainu who has ever been to the United States. I spent a year in San Francisco once." In 1897 or so, when he was seventeen years old, he had been hired on board a Japanese sealing ship as rifleman. "We Ainu had the best shooting eye around here, and all the Japanese sealers wanted us to work for them." One day they were boarded by an American Coast Guard vessel for some suspected violation. "All those *shamo* (the Ainu word for 'dirty Japs') pointed to us and said it was our fault. Of course, we didn't know what it was all about. We were taken off the sealer and put aboard the American ship, and then we were taken to Alaska." Since it was deep winter, they spent the season there living in a small post where there were many Eskimo. "What did you think of the Eskimo?" I asked, delighted at this choice anthropological tidbit, the encounter of Ainu and Eskimo.

"Well," he thought back, "you know, their music is like ours. But they look just like the damn Japs."

When winter had thawed into spring, they were taken to San Francisco for trial. San Francisco was the first modern city they had ever seen. At home, they had never even gone as far as Sapporo, the capital of Hokkaido, not to speak of Tokyo. Traveled they were, but always on long voyages to remote, bleak, north-

ern waters; their only stopovers were in tiny fishing settlements in the Kuriles or on the northeast coast of Hokkaido.
"San Francisco," he recalled, "was all mountains and light. I
had never seen anything so bright. I had never seen such tall
buildings. At first we were frightened." After about one year
they were placed aboard a Japanese ship bound for Yokohama.
This was also a first for them: Yokohama. They were given
some money and a rail ticket for Hokkaido, and after a few days
in Tokyo, another first—"much bigger than San Francisco," he
said, "but not so bright"—they finally returned to Usu.

His narrative was accompanied by a great deal of drinking,
and soon he and his friends began to warm up. They formed a
circle and began to sing, using an Ainu drum and a standard
Japanese shamisen, or three-stringed lute, for accompaniment
and clapping out the rhythm by hand. As spirits rose, several
began to get up to dance. Occasionally someone perfunctorily
explained what the song or dance was about, and my Japanese
associates eagerly stalked them with questions, carefully inscrib-
ing the answers in notebooks they had drawn out of the flowing
sleeves of their *yukata*, the lightweight kimono that is worn for
relaxing in the evening and for sleeping. "This is the fellow who
was with me in San Francisco," my friend called out, introducing an even older man, just past the threshold of senility. He
grinned aimlessly and continued to stand there, not sure of
what had been said, knowing only that it had something to do
with him. While the men were reaching the stage of waxy flexi-
bility, an old lady came over to teach me an Ainu song. Just as I
was starting to repeat the words, I felt a tap on my shoulder.

"May I speak to you a moment?" a young man in steel-
rimmed glasses asked me, his expression located somewhere
between proper respectfulness and controlled anger. "In the
next room," he said. I followed him into the next room, which
was separated from our chamber only by thin, paper sliding
doors. There I found two other young men, like him wearing
jacket and tie and seated stiffly around a low Japanese table.
The party sounds were almost as loud as if we were still in the

next room. "We are here to protest your making a spectacle of these old people," the young man who had tapped my shoulder said immediately.

"I don't understand," I started, confused by the sudden change of pace.

"You are deliberately getting them drunk to make them do those barbaric songs and dances. We would like you to stop immediately. It's an insult to us. You are making a spectacle of us, treating us as barbarians," someone said.

It's because of people like you, keeping these old things alive just to satisfy your curiosity, that discrimination continues." (This was the first time I had ever heard the word "discrimination," much as it would have been used about American blacks.) "I am as good a Japanese as anyone else here. I served in the army and several of my friends, from this very village, died in the war. The only difference is that my ancestors spoke a different language. But that doesn't make me different from other Japanese. In the past, every part of this country had its own dialect. Today we all speak standard Japanese. But every Japanese, not just us, has ancestors who spoke a different dialect. Our dialect happens to have been called Ainu. But like everybody else, we have progressed, and now we want the old dialect to disappear so that we can stand up as equals."

"Look," I said, "I can't call off this party and send back people who have come here in good faith. If you are so worried about their misbehaving, why don't you join us?"

He looked at me frostily. "I see we cannot get any place with you. But I want you to know that you are offending all Ainu youth in this community by this performance. You are deliberately trying to degrade us."

I went back into the party room, but the spirit was going out of things. Everybody had heard our argument through the thin partition. Two of the old men were completely drunk and one of the old ladies was trying to shake them upright. "They do get drunk easily," observed one of the Japanese researchers, making some marks in his notebook. The party soured to its end.

Over the next few days, I had several meetings with these young Ainu and their friends. In the end they forgave me for "not knowing any better" and accepted my assurances that my intentions had been honorable. I, in turn, came to understand their agony. They faced the same dilemma that all despised minority groups do, especially those not strong enough to control their own destinies: assimilation or preservation of their identity. These young men were desperate to assimilate, to become Japanese. "In two generations," one argued, "this whole problem will become part of history. We will all be Japanese. The Ainu memory will fade away, unless it is deliberately kept alive. That's why we were so angry at you the other night. You were doing just what those *shamo*, who despise us, always do. They would rather have us continue as a quaint, primitive enclave, to be stared at and to be felt superior to, rather than become equals."

Was this what all of old man Bachelor's labor of love had ended up in? He had brought them Christianity, education, and modern aspirations so that they could enter the mainstream of Japanese life on equal terms, but they could do this only by rejecting the other prong of his offering: pride in being an Ainu. Many years later, in the late 1970s, when I ran across a political pamphlet signed "Ainu Liberation League" and then learned that they had run a candidate in Japan's Upper House election (he lost), this conversation of more than thirty years earlier returned to me, and I imagined the activists of the Ainu Liberation League Looking rather like the young men whom I had met in Daté-Monbetsu.

The ex-Baron Daté

"You haven't met our lord yet," one of the fishery cooperative officials said to us. "He'll be able to see you tonight." In Japan of 1947, hip-deep in the American Occupation's "democratization" program, the old-fashioned word, *tonosama*, which had been used in feudal times for the domain lord, rang with an odd echo. I know that there was still a resident Daté descendant of the cadet branch of the lords of Sendai who had first taken on the official commission to colonize this area. He had been, if not the largest of the landowners, still a landlord and certainly the town's leading citizen. Until the abolition of the peerage system required by the Occupation's democratization reforms, he had held the title of baron. In the spring of 1947, he had just finished a three-year term of office as mayor. He was also, I learned, a *yōshi*, that is, an adopted husband.

This practice of adopting husbands is probably unique to Japan. It works as follows: when a family has no sons, or when the sons are for some reason not suitable as heirs, a promising young man is adopted. In order to do this, he sheds his original family name and takes his wife's name. This is to assure physical continuity, that the family will not die out for lack of sons or because the blood heir was insane or incapable of carrying out the family responsibilities.

But whatever the advantages for the family system itself, being an adopted son was not the most desirable of fates. An old Japanese proverb advises the young man to avoid becoming a *yōshi* as long as he has "even three grains of bran." The reason is that the *yōshi* takes on what is usually the feminine role. In traditional Japanese conception, the bride "leaves" her home. Her name is struck from her family's register and inscribed on her new family's. As a member of a strange family, she goes to live in the home of her husband—who had usually been until then a stranger—where she comes under the control of her mother-in-law. She must learn to get along with her, to please and obey her, and to transform herself to conform to what her new family considers proper. We have our mother-in-law jokes, but in Japan the mother-in-law is "worse than a thousand tigers." And so are the older sisters of the husband, the "little mothers-in-law," who can also order the bride about.

In the *yōshi* marriage, the situation is reversed. It is the husband who must submit himself to his wife's family's authority. He leaves his own family (and has his name stricken from the register), he takes on his wife's name, he lives in her home with her family, and he is the one who must make himself acceptable to them. If disputes arise, he knows her family will side against him. He must tread lightly, accommodate himself, suppress his normal impulses as a Japanese male to take a strong line with his wife.

The ex-Baron Daté was a *yōshi*. The continuity of the family, the relation to the family's past, the sense of family pride resided with his wife, even though he was the legal heir. Everyone, however, spoke well, even warmly, of him. He did not sound like the overbearing, arrogant feudal lord, the landowner of caricature oppressing his tenants. Partly, I realized, this was because so many of the local people were of samurai descent, only three generations or so away from the original samurai settlers from the Sendai domain. But one sensed a more personal warmth than could be accounted for solely by this fact.

He had not, it turned out, been one of the larger landlords. On the contrary, his holdings were rather modest. Furthermore, he had not only accepted the land reform but had also played a role in making it more palatable to some of the other landlords. Most notable of all, he and his wife had kept a small piece of their own land for themselves and had become dirt farmers like everybody else. Under the land reform law, resident landlords were permitted to retain a small portion of their lands if they wished to cultivate it themselves. In many parts of Japan this "reserved land," as it was called, had been one of the more controversial issues of the reform. But not in Daté-Monbetsu. The willingness of the Baron Daté and his noble wife to become farmers was a matter of pride, rather than the usual source of litigious contest before the local land commission.

I wanted to see this prodigy. I had been for some time looking into problems of land reform all over Japan, and I was aware of the fact that in general it was the smaller, rather than the larger, landowners who resisted most bitterly. The great landowners were often men of a certain nobility of vision. Sometimes their sense of community responsibility led them not only to acquiesce gracefully but to play an active role in making the reform a success.

The most endearing example I knew was one of the four great landlords of Niigata Prefecture. He was glad to lay down the burdens, he had told me. "It was too much work. We had to keep it going because of our hereditary responsibilities, even though we were losing money on our lands." When I met him, soon after the start of the land reform, he had just converted his estate house into a Museum of Northern Culture and himself moved out into an adjoining small house. "This is the way I have always wanted to live," he told me enthusiastically, his avuncular face creased by a thousand wrinkles, all of them smiling. "I have always wanted to be the curator of a museum. What better way can I serve my people than by helping to elevate their educational level and bring them some pride in their history. It is also a way of paying tribute to my own ancestors."

At that time, he had already set up his first exhibits, based entirely on the treasures and relics of his family—armor, weapons, saddlery, pictures, scrolls, historical records, chests, desks, books, ceremonial garments, lacquerware, inkstones. For the future, he had planned a series of exhibits, starting with one on "The Culture of Northern Life," centering around a traditional household, the everyday utensils of kitchen and field, clothing for daily and ceremonial wear. For a later date, he was planning a more ambitious exhibit to illustrate the history of the area's colonization: the wars with the Ainu, in pictures and documents; the armor, saddles, swords, lances, spears, daggers, clubs; the early tools for cultivation; the crops. He was like an enthusiastic young boy and enjoyed nothing better than talking about his plans for the museum. He would make the rounds of his ex-tenants (who numbered over one hundred families), this time not to collect rents or dispense lordly wisdom, but to exhort them to send their children to the museum. He had already invited several anthropologists to advise him, was negotiating for a technical director (he planned modestly to be the assistant director), and had fluttered his Tokyo contacts for financial support.

Another great landlord, who ruled a domain on the Japan Sea side that was one of the most classically feudal, was a graduate of Kyoto Imperial University's Faculty of Economics. "My grandfather and my father always told me," he said to me, sitting over his potter's wheel (he was an ardent amateur potter with his own installation, including wheels, kiln, and workshop, and a friend of most of the great potters of Japan), "the day of the great landowner is coming to an end. And don't forget, I also studied modern economics. So I am neither surprised nor unprepared." And indeed he was not. The land reform had taken away his cultivated lands, but it left him his great holdings of forest, then the largest private holdings in Japan. In fact, there is some reason to believe that the land reform was far from an unmixed curse: it relieved him of heavy losses by putting an end to his seigneurial responsibilities to his tenants and to the village.

Many of the great landowners remained wealthy men. If they lost their lands, they retained forest holdings, or their business interests, or their local industrial or commercial enterprises. All over the country, large landlords could be found starting forest-based industries, such as woodworking or lumbering, or bringing entirely new industries to their home villages. Partly this was to reconstruct their own fortunes, and partly it was to provide jobs for the community. But the small and medium landowners, the holders of half an acre to three acres, who had no other source of income, were the ones who howled most. Some were elderly people who had retired on their tiny acres, others had sunk their life savings into land as an investment only to have it taken away from them.

It was not surprising therefore that a baron of the House of Daté should have responded to the land reform with *noblesse*. What was surprising was that he should have become a farmer.

We arrived at the Daté home about seven in the evening. It was a large, traditional mansion, already seedy from lack of at-

168

tention. "We had to let all of our servants go," the baroness explained apologetically. The entryway led into a series of chambers and then into a large hall, two stories high. A balconied walk ran along the second floor, and all around the walk there were fitted cabinets, some of them with drawers and closets, but many, I noticed, long and narrow, like map cabinets.

Seated on the polished wood floor of the balcony were the baron and baroness dressed in peasant work clothes. They were polishing swords. She would hand him a sword, and he would draw it gently from its scabbard and oil it with a rag, careful not to touch it with his hand. Then he would pass it to her. She would apply powder with a large puff and then again return the sword to him to polish. "Sorry to meet you this way," he said, hardly looking up, "but we have to get this done." They continued their buffing and polishing, taking each sword out of its cabinet, inspecting it carefully along the line of the blade after the polishing was complete, and then returning it to the cabinet. This went on for about five more swords, when finally they put the last one away, patted the powder from their hands and clothes, and turned to be properly sociable with us. We joined them on the floor of the balcony, and tea and sweetcakes were served.

The baron was a man of gentle looks, soft, tender eyes, and very restrained movements. He spoke softly and only when directly questioned. Often he looked lost, as if bewildered by all the attention. His wife acted much more in command, answering many of the questions and sometimes even volunteering information. Even in her heavy layers of shapeless clothing, she had an ineffable, almost a fey, nobility about her. Her eyes smiled easily, as if she were vastly amused at our discomfiture and ponderousness. Sometimes one had the feeling that she was trying to make it clear that she was the Daté, not he; at other times, that she was trying to shield him from too much painful probing.

They both looked tired, although as proper Japanese they

promptly denied the suggestion. They held their bodies straight and attentive. "He's a bit tired," she said later, nodding toward her husband. "We've been in the fields since early this morning. And, of course, we're not quite used to it yet." Every day, as soon as they returned from the fields, they had immediately to sit down to work on their swords for several hours. The Daté heirlooms were a collection of more than thirty swords, dating from hundreds of years before. Several of them were formally classified as Important Cultural Objects, and under the laws concerning national treasures, the owners were required to follow specified procedures in taking care of them, on penalty of having them removed by the government.

There is a highly developed philosophy, a mystique, about Japanese swords. The great ones have a living quality and personality that distinguish them from all others. They become living things, almost gods to be worshiped. Their relation to their owners has a mystic quality that is only vaguely suggested to us by the legends of King Arthur's knights with their Excaliburs. Swordmaking was virtually a priestly profession. To make their swords, the smiths had to keep themselves in a state of ritual purity. Before starting his work the swordsmith will —even today—go through a preparatory period of abstinence and purification. When he is ready to start, he cleanses himself with lustrations of cold water, puts on ceremonial robes, and makes obeisance before the altar of his protecting deity.

The makers and names of the great swords are household words, and their histories are matters of common knowledge. The Devil-Cutter, for example, was the treasured sword of Yoshisada Nitta, the great warrior of the fourteenth century, who was finally defeated by his erstwhile ally, Takauji Ashikaga, the founder of the Ashikaga line of shoguns. Takauji's own favorite sword was the Bone-Cutter. In the eleventh century, Monju of Michinoku made two swords for Mitsunaka of the House of Minamoto. The blades were tested, as was a common practice, on corpses: one sliced through the beard and clean through the body, so it was called the Beard-Cutter, the other

170

proved itself out through the knee, so it was called the Knee-Cutter. Other famous swords were given names like Stone-Cutter, Fog on the River, Little Fox, The Eel, The Little Crow, and so on, based upon their special qualities or particular incidents.

The greatest of all was the Heavenly Cloud Mass, one of the Three Imperial Treasures (the other two are the Sacred Mirror and the Sacred Jewel). According to legend, the storm god, Susano-o, found this sword in the tail of the eight-forked dragon with which he did battle. It was given to the Emperor Jimmu, the legendary founder of the imperial line, as one of the three sacred treasures. During the reign of the tenth of the earthly emperors, the sword, along with the other treasures, was deposited in the Grand Shrine of Isé by the Princess Yamato Himé no Mikoto. A copy of the sword was made and also deposited in the Isé Shrine. In 1185, when the eighty-first emperor, then still a child, drowned during the naval battle of Dannoura, the sword that went to the bottom with him was the copy, not the original, as had been feared.

The sword is the soldier's honor, the reflection of his soul. To part with it or to stain it is to lose his honor, to stain his reputation. It must be kept brightly polished. During the period of military rule, which lasted from the end of the twelfth century until 1868, the sword was the symbol of the warrior's status. A samurai wore his two swords as a badge of rank; commoners were forbidden to wear them, unless specifically awarded the privilege.

The Japanese swords of the thirteenth and fourteenth centuries were probably the greatest ever produced in the world, greater even than the fabled blades of Damascus and Toledo. The Daté swords were prized family heirlooms, symbols of the family's history and honor, as well as art objects. The greatest was Nagamitsu, or "Long Radiance" (also called Azuki, or "Red Bean"), made in the thirteenth century. This officially designated Important Cultural Object, which measures about two-and-a-half feet long, was a glittering hand-forged blade that

171

could cut a man, and perhaps his horse, in two with one stroke. It had come to the Daté family as a reciprocal wedding gift from Lord Uesugi of the Echigo Domain when one of the Daté sons went there as an adopted son. The other great treasure was a *tantō*, or "short sword," in the iris pattern made by Sadayoshi in the fourteenth century. Each of the other swords, although not boasting so exalted a classification, had its own unique history, quality, and beauty.

In order to keep up with them, the Daté had to oil, buff, and polish several every day. This they could only do after they had finished working in the fields. "Why did you decide to become a farmer?" I asked him. "We had no other way to make a living," he explained. "We decided that if we were going to lose our lands, we would rather stay here and make our living than leave the community." "Our first worry," his wife told us, "was how to take care of our dependents. People in our position have many hereditary retainers and we can't let them down. But now most of them are settled." They were planning, the baron explained, to give up the big house and to build a small one more in accord with their new situation.

"Are you going to sell all these art treasures?" I asked them.

"Oh, no," the baroness replied, shocked. "These are not for sale. We'll probably give them to the town. Maybe they can make a museum." (Several years later they did, in fact, give the house and the art treasures to the city as a museum.) What did he plan to do? I asked the baron. "Nothing," he replied, "just live quietly. I have no political ambitions; I don't want to hold office. I just finished three years as mayor and I never want to do it again. That's for the others to do."

The local officials accompanying us moved about with exaggerated respectfulness, beaming with pride. "You see what a fine lord we have here," they said later.

That was thirty-five years ago. Since then, much has changed. But that is another story.

VII ✩

A BALANCE SHEET

Falling in Love

Herewith ends the first phase of my encounter with Japan. I do not mean that I had become an expert, or even that I knew a great deal. Far from it. But for the first time I felt that I had stepped over that mysterious threshold that separates the rank learner from whatever the next stage is.

Let me be more exact. The first subphase ended in the late spring of 1946—before the events I describe in the last chapter—that is, when I was transferred from Fukuoka to Tokyo.

The second subphase, which began in Kyoto the early summer of 1946, lies outside the frame of this book. Very briefly, I had managed through some adroit bureaucratic maneuvering to spend four or five weeks in Kyoto, and it was during this time that the "something" happened to me that my old Japan-hand army buddy had assured me would happen. Until then I had found Japan interesting. But it was only when I went to Kyoto for the first time that I felt something more. Suddenly I was engaged, gripped, as if in some strange way I had actually become part of the scene. I don't know if "falling in love" is the

173

right term for this, but if by falling in love we mean feeling oneself in a destined relation with someone or something, being so involved that what one does makes a difference to others and what happens to others makes a difference to oneself, then it is correct to say that I fell in love with Japan.

The external events are only markers along the path of that inner development. Kyoto was for me at first only a place to ease the eye and spirit after the destruction that I encountered everywhere else in Japan. To leave Tokyo on the overnight sleeper train and arrive early in the morning in Kyoto was to take a step back in history, to enter another world entirely. Suddenly there were old buildings standing intact, a reminder of what Japan had once been and of how life must have been lived in the settings that were now so totally disrupted by the war. It is not that Kyoto people were entirely spared the postwar shortages and suffering. But by comparison with Tokyo and Yokohama and Fukuoka, not to speak of Hiroshima and Nagasaki, theirs was a haven of peace. Houses stood intact, people had clothes to wear, and a gentle tranquillity, even if somewhat tinged with anxiety, still ruled the streets and homes. Kyoto was a far cry from the rest of urban Japan.

Going to Kyoto was an escape, a blessed release from the hassle and the harsh suffering that constantly assailed the eyes elsewhere. The sense of contrast was further heightened by the fact that much of the time I was able to stay not in the Kyoto Hotel, which was the usual billet for lower-level Occupation personnel on travel status, but in one of Kyoto's loveliest estates, the Mitsubishi mansion at the foot of Higashiyama, the "Eastern Mountain." Three families were then living there, executives of the Mitsubishi Bank who had been repatriated from overseas at the end of the war and had, for the moment, no other place to live. The place was a dream Japanese palace, with many large rooms, a moon-viewing room, a Japanese garden replete with a small waterfall, a teahouse, and an English garden flush up against the mountain. Higashiyama was part of the scenery and, for the first time, I learned the meaning of the term *shakkei*, "borrowed scenery," in Japanese landscape gardening.

Unfortunately, the Mitsubishi estate was such a desirable property that it was not long before the local military government team decided to requisition it as a residence for several Occupation families. The requisitioning was one thing— although I was furious about having my private dream world taken away; my own view was that the estate should have been left as a preserve, an enclave of beauty, like the temples and shrines of Kyoto. But what they did to it, to make it suitable for several Western families to live in, was to my mind a desecration. Straw tatami were ripped out and replaced by wooden floors, to be covered by carpets and trodden by shoes, the sliding paper doors were replaced by walls and doors, and the rooms were cut up or enlarged without regard to the original aesthetic conceptions that underlay them. The ultimate desecration, it seemed to me, was the conversion of the moon-viewing room into a Western-style sun parlor crammed with rattan furniture and children's playthings. One of the two lawns, I was told, was eliminated and the area sodded over to supply a turf for golf practice. Or was it a space for children to play? I don't remember.

But I do remember wailing, "How could you people do this?" to a friend of mine, a member of the local military government team. He was a young man, in his early twenties, also a product of one of the army language schools, and he regarded himself as a "progressive intellectual." (Later he went into a somewhat nonstandard academic career, basically not concerned with Japan; but before going off to more distant fields, he wrote an interesting book attacking Occupation policy in his own area of activity.) "The hell with them," was his response. "Why should we worry about these guys? The *zaibatsu* are responsible for the war, and they deserve anything we do to them." When I argued that it was a question of putting Philistine hands to a thing of beauty, not of punishing the *zaibatsu*, his eyes sparkled vengefully and he repeated, "Why are you so sentimental about these old Japanese houses? These guys are getting just what they deserve. If I had my way, I'd rip the whole thing down and build a public housing project for workers."

For many years this experience remained for me a symbol of vulgar American insensitivity and bad taste. But recently, when I see the general debasement of Japanese taste, the massive abandonment of traditional aesthetic standards, and the low level of modern housing and interior decoration, I wonder if my reaction of the time was justified. Would not most modern Japanese do exactly the same thing to beautiful old houses that the Kyoto military government team did to the Mitsubishi mansion in 1946? There is nothing unusual about a Japanese family today stuffing traditional rooms with furniture, cutting up open spaces into small rooms, throwing rugs and carpets on tatami floors, converting a moon-viewing room into a playroom for children, and paving over a garden area with concrete to provide play space for the children or an area for hanging laundry. I can no longer criticize my friend in my mind as self-righteously as I did then.

On the fourth of July, 1946, a large group of Occupation personnel, plus Japanese aides, guides, coworkers, and friends, spent a memorable night at Kyoto's most famous geisha house, the Ichiriki, in the Gion geisha district. Who paid for all this, I do not remember, although in those days Americans could actually afford such things. Or if not, then the bills would be picked up in one way or another. A fresh "apprentice geisha," a *maiko*, was trotted out for us, and I remember that we were all very drunk. A WAC sergeant, who normally suppressed her mildly lesbian inclinations, began competing with the men for the *maiko*'s attention. The night was a milestone in many ways—among others, that for the first time I drank two full liters of saké all by myself. As I wobbled my jeep drunkenly through the dark streets of Kyoto, nimbly evading the MP patrols on the lookout for curfew violators, I felt that I had indeed arrived in Japan.

My army buddies, whatever their assignments might have

been, have similar experiences to relate. All of them, in one manner or another, passed through their initiation period, and most of them succeeded in penetrating the mystic barrier that separates Phase One from Phase Two. The question that arises is whether these experiences had any significance other than the purely personal.

Language Officers

The original purpose of the Army Intensive Japanese Language School—and of its navy counterpart—was to train a large cadre of language officers capable of handling the enemy language well enough to serve as combat intelligence officers in the field. Their function was to be the handling of prisoners, the interrogation of prisoners for intelligence purposes, the reading of enemy documents, and appealing to enemy troops to surrender. While most of them were expected to serve in the combat areas, some were expected to make use of their skills behind the lines, in headquarters, in the Signal Corps, in cryptography, and in analyzing enemy broadcasts, newspapers, and captured documents.

It is questionable whether the language program succeeded, at least in the way it was intended to. One simple reason was that it did not produce enough language officers for the tasks that needed doing. Altogether, the army school completed the training of less than eight hundred language officers (that is, non-Japanese-Americans). By the end of the Pacific War, this number had reached no more than five hundred, and only a small proportion of them had reached the combat areas. The rest were still in the pipeline—in school, awaiting shipment to the Pacific, or in rear-echelon positions such as Hawaii and Australia awaiting further advance into the combat zones. Effectively, one can assume that at any given moment in time there were only a few hundred in the field. As against the number of combat areas, clearly this number was inadequate; most combat units operated all or most of the war without the service of language officers.

The addition of the navy officers does not change the picture significantly. The Navy Japanese Language School trained some one thousand two hundred language officers. But the same proportions prevailed as between the noncombat—those still in training, in the pipelines, in rear-echelon units, and aboard ship—and the combat numbers. The number available for direct combat contact with the enemy as, say, in the marine landings in the Pacific islands, was very limited.

Another reason is that not all of the language officers were equally good in Japanese. Many of them could not handle Japanese at a level equal to the heavy demands of the combat situation. The usual procedure in the army was to place one language officer in charge of a combat language team of approximately ten Nisei. Therefore, the bulk of the combat intelligence was carried by the Nisei rather than by the language officers. This situation, as we have already seen, caused difficulties back in Camp Savage and Fort Snelling, where Nisei felt they were being discriminated against. And reports from the field enhanced the feeling of unfairness. Many of the Nisei felt that their own Japanese was much better than that of their officers, and in some cases they were downright contemptuous of the officers' language ability.

Since the navy had no language personnel other than non-Japanese-Americans, navy officers in the field had also to be assigned to combat language teams consisting of Nisei soldiers.

It would, therefore, be very difficult to come to any definitive conclusions about how successful this aspect of the military language training programs was. They produced some good officers, who in fact performed well the functions they were expected to perform, but they produced many others who did not. Since this was wartime, it was not unreasonable to expect some waste. The military had no alternative, given the situation and their own view of the possibilities, but to train as many people as possible and then hope that a decent percentage would turn out well and perform usefully. The alternative, of relying entirely on Japanese-Americans, with perhaps a little backup from the

BIJs, universities, or other special language programs, simply did not occur to the military as a possibility at the beginning of the war. And once the system started out, it could not be changed in midstream.

Although at the start of the language program very few people were thinking that far ahead, there was a vague expectation that after the war the language officers would play if not the key role then certainly an important role in the Occupation of Japan. The same question arises, however, as to whether they in fact did. There was, as I have already indicated with regard to their combat role, the matter of sheer numbers. Of the approximately two thousand language officers trained during the war, far less than half can be assumed to have taken any part in the Occupation at all. No exact figures are available on how many actually served, but there are strong reasons to doubt that it was as much as one-third. In the first place, large numbers found themselves at the end of the war with enough points of service to be discharged from the armed forces immediately. The earlier classes were all in this position. Even the language officers who came to Japan directly from combat or advance-echelon positions at the end of the war, remained only a short while and then returned to civilian life. During this short stay they were usually with the combat unit to which they had been assigned and never took part in the Occupation operation as such. In the case of my own class, which was the second from the last in the army program, just over one-half of the class refused to be commissioned and secured discharges from the army without coming to Japan. A small number of those discharged eventually made their way to Japan during the Occupation, but the vast majority simply returned to civilian life without ever having made use of their training. An even larger number of the final Fort Snelling class, the one that followed mine, took this course. And one can assume that it was approximately the same for the navy language officers.

And here again there was the question of degree of language skill. Some of the officers were good, others poor. Those whose postgraduation experience placed them in a position to use the language improved their skills, while those who supervised teams of Nisei, or remained in rear-echelon positions requiring little use of their language found their skills quickly withering away.

Quite apart from numbers and language ability, however, another factor became of great importance in connection with the Occupation: professional skills. Most of the language officers were young, not yet fully launched on their professions. They therefore had little, other than language, to offer to the Occupation. But as it turned out, language was not the crying need. The Occupation first depended primarily on the Japanese-Americans, both in and out of uniform, and then later increasingly on the Japanese themselves. Despite the enormous American effort and the wartime slowdown in Japan, there were still far more Japanese who spoke English than Americans who spoke Japanese. In the encounters between the Occupation and the Japanese, it was normally the Japanese side that provided the interpreters. Every staff section of the Occupation had its Japanese employees to take care of language matters, from interpreting to the translation of documents and the carrying on of administrative work in Japanese.

It was this situation that gave rise to the widespread charge that Occupation officers were overly dependent on their interpreters and that therefore the interpreters had an undue influence. Harry Emerson Wildes, an old Japan hand who served in the Occupation's Government Section, entitled one chapter of his book, *Typhoon in Tokyo*, "Rule by Interpreters." This was, to some extent, justified. Sometimes an Occupation officer's estimate of Japanese public opinion about one or another issue was based upon nothing more substantial than what he was told by his Japanese staff or associates, rather like the quickie expert foreign correspondent who sizes up the state of public opinion in a country he is visiting for the first time by what his taxi driver from airport to hotel tells him. There has been much talk about all the Americanisms that the Occupation forced the Japanese to translate literally into the postwar Constitution; but it is equally worth noting that many of the Occupation's reforms reflected both the language and the ideas of Japanese experts who worked as staff members or advisors to the Occupation staff sections.

Very few of the language officers found their way into policy-making or substantive positions. This was by no means, of course, universally the case. Some of them ended up in positions for which they were well suited in terms of skill and experience.

The most glamorous assignment, it seemed to us in the early period, was that of the writer Faubion Bowers. He ended up the war as a major and a personal aide to General MacArthur. As if this were not already glamor enough to last a lifetime, on top of that Bowers managed to have himself transferred from MacArthur's side to the position of theater censor. His area was the Kabuki, which had already engaged his interest before the war.

In the early period of the Occupation, the Kabuki theater was placed under severe censorship. It was regarded as embodying "feudal" and ultranationalistic values and was therefore ideologically suspect. All Kabuki plays, no matter how impeccably classic, that seemed to the Occupation to be patriotic or to support the military ethos, were banned from public performance. Plays of revenge, or plays showing open scenes of strife, bloodshed, or death were censored as "feudal." This meant that such classics as *Chūshingura* ("A Treasury of Loyal Retainers") could not be shown. When Bowers took over as Kabuki censor, he changed all this and his encouragement of the revival of the great classics played an important role in keeping the Kabuki from going down the drain, as it seemed for a while to be in danger of doing the first few years after the war. To me, this was an enviable assignment—to deal with culture and to be able to overcome narrow-minded prejudice and restore historical perspective and humanistic criteria to the situation. Later, Bowers was followed in this post by two other lucky members of our company, Earl Ernst, a professor of drama at the University of Hawaii (and later the translator of several Kabuki and Noh plays), and a high school teacher from New York, a man of highly developed intellectual and cultural interests.

Many years later, a controversy arose over the role that Bowers had played in the postwar development of the Kabuki theater. The famous female impersonator, Baiko Onoe, in a recent book *Ume to kiku* ("Plum and Chrysanthemum"), is very favorable, but the equally famous female impersonator, Kunitarō, in his book of reminiscences *Oyama no michi hitosuji* ("The Straight Road of the Female Impersonator"), evaluates his role more negatively, on the grounds that his support of the revival of the classics discouraged the development of new creations for the Kabuki theater.

There were other happy assignments as well. Kurt Steiner, today professor of political science at Stanford University, played an important role in the Legal Section of the Occupation, working on the reform of the legal codes. Then a recent Austrian refugee, his training in continental law turned out to be peculiarly appropriate to the job because Japanese law was based on continental European rather than Anglo-Saxon models. Hans Baerwald, today professor of political science at the University of California, Los Angeles, was in the Political Section of the Occupation; his doctoral dissertation (*The Purge of Japanese Leaders under the Occupation*, Berkeley, University of California Press, 1959) was an analysis of the purges, a program in which he himself had taken part. Solis Horwitz, from my own class, who had been a professor of law at the University of Pittsburgh and a practicing attorney in civilian life, became one of the top prosecutors in the war crimes trials; he later wrote what remained for many years the most important single account of the trials in English. A member of the first Company A class at the University of Michigan served on the defense side of the same trials; he later became one of the few foreigners allowed to practice law in Japan.

There were not many exceptions, but fortunately, at least for myself, I was one of them. Fukuoka had not been a bad posting,

182

and I had gained a great deal from my stay there. But however
good it may have been for my own education, I did not relish
the prospect of spending the rest of my military career censoring telegrams. After about four months of this life, one of the
top officers of our language school came through Fukuoka and
interviewed me. He knew from my record that I was not only an
anthropologist but that I had had public opinion experience as
well, and he offered to look around for some suitable professional work for me to do. What came through was a reassign-
ment to the Civil Information and Education Section of SCAP
(Supreme Command for the Allied Powers) in Tokyo, to help in
the development of public opinion research.

My predecessor in that position was a Marine Corps major
who was a fellow anthropologist and had studied Japanese (as
well as Chinese) at Harvard University before the war. We
overlapped for several weeks before he finally left in order to be
discharged from the services and return to his doctoral course
at Harvard. Shortly thereafter, I managed to persuade my commanding officer that our mission should be enlarged to include
the wider social background of public opinion. As a result, we
became the Public Opinion and Sociological Research Division
(PO & SR). In my wildest dreams, I could never have concocted
a better job for myself at that particular stage of my life.

But I was one of the few exceptions. Most of the language
school graduates were concentrated in a limited number of
places in the Occupation, primarily in the language services
(Allied Translators and Interpreters Service, or ATIS) and information and intelligence services (counterintelligence, G-2, and
criminal investigation). The language officers played a modest
role in the Occupation; their real contribution was elsewhere.

Lessons

If the program did not fully succeed in the things it set out to
do, it was successful in two unexpected ways: first, in the establishment of the scholarly field of Japanese studies after the war;
second, in the creation of a cadre of men who for a long time

played an important part in Japanese-American relations.

At that time, we did not, of course, realize what was happening. But the fact is that we were involved in what eventually turned out to have been an important episode in the intellectual history of our times: the creation of a new field of studies in American and, as a consequence, in world scholarship. Before the war, there had been in the United States only a handful of institutions and a tiny band of scholars dedicated to Japan studies. In the rest of the world—Japan's colonies excepted—there was almost nothing. But within a few years after the conclusion of the war, the field of Japanology erupted. Dozens of universities began to offer a specialization in Japan studies, and hundreds for the first time began offering courses in Japanese and Far Eastern history, society, literature, language, and the arts. The largest proportion of those who manned these programs came in the first instance from among the graduates of the army and navy language schools.

How many of the language school graduates went into the academic world and remained involved in Japan, it would be hard to say. A number of calculations I have made, however, suggests that a figure of slightly under one-fifth, most of them dealing with Japan, would not be far wrong. This means that the wartime language schools contributed somewhere between three hundred and four hundred academics, of whom between one hundred and fifty and two hundred and fifty were involved in one degree or another with Japan. Together they have so far produced over two thousand books on Japan (plus some other subjects) and tens of thousands of articles. Whether such an outpouring is to be counted a blessing or a curse, there can be no question that it has had great influence on several generations of Japan specialists, on hundreds of thousands of ordinary students, on policy makers, and on the general public.

Scholars who went through Company A include anthropologists John Cornell (Texas), Edward Norbeck (Rice), George De Vos (California, Berkeley), Paul Bohannon, William Mulloy (Wyoming), Robert McKnight (California, Heyward),

184

and Walter Fairservis (American Museum of Natural History); political scientists Joseph Sutton (former president of the University of Indiana, now deceased), Hans Baerwald (UCLA), Ernest Haas (California, Berkeley), Wesley Fisher (Michigan State, now deceased), Fred Kerlinger, Carl Lande (Kansas), John Montgomery (Harvard), Gaston Sigur (George Washington), Kurt Steiner (Stanford), Rodger Swearingen (UCLA), Robert Textor, Richard Sneider (Columbia); historians Robert Spaulding (Oklahoma State), William Chambliss (Kentucky), Conrad Brant, Robert Butow (Washington), George Lensen (Florida State, deceased), Arthur Tiedemann (City University of New York and Columbia), George Totten (Southern California), and Grant Goodman (Kansas); geographers David Kornhauser (Hawaii) and John Eyre (North Carolina); legal scholars Dan F. Henderson (Washington) and Solis Horwitz (Pittsburgh, deceased); arts specialists James Cahill (California, Berkeley) and Harold Stern (director of the Freer Gallery); language, literature, and thought specialists Robert Brower (Michigan), Donald Bailey (Arizona), William Arrowsmith (Johns Hopkins), Leon Hurwitz (British Columbia), William Booth (Chico State, California), Paul Diesing, Robert Langbauer (Virginia), Wayne Oxford, Philip Jenner (Hawaii), Harry Schneidwind (Detroit) and Edward Copeland (Minnesota); and sociologist Norman Jacobs (Illinois).

A corresponding list could as easily be drawn up for the navy graduates: anthropologist Richard Beardsley (Michigan, deceased); literature, language, and thought specialists Donald Keene, W. Theodore de Bary, Edward Seidensticker (Columbia), Donald Shively (Harvard), Roy Miller (Washington), Frank Gibney (Encyclopaedia Britannica); historians Thomas Smith (California, Berkeley), Otis Cary (Dōshisha), John W. Hall, Robert Schwantes, Delmar Brown (California, Berkeley) and Roger Hackett (Michigan); economist Jerome Cohen (retired, City University of New York); and political scientists Robert Ward (Stanford), James Morley (Columbia), and William Henderson.

☆   A small number of distinguished Japanologists came through some of the smaller service programs. Marius Jansen (Princeton) studied at Harvard's CAT (Civil Affairs Training) school, and Howard Hibbett, Japanese literature (Harvard) and Benjamin Schwartz, Chinese thought (Harvard) both studied in the Army Signal Corps program at Arlington Hall. But these two programs were not as intensive as the navy and army programs.

The army's Military Intelligence Service Language School also provided training to about six thousand Nisei. Since the Nisei were not selected for their academic qualification primarily, not many of them went into academic life, but the group that has done so has attained some distinction, both in Japan studies and in other fields.

The service schools made another important contribution: to U.S.–Japan relations. For the first period after the war, the fact that there was a cadre of Americans able to speak Japanese and to communicate with important publics in the United States played a major role. In the following decades, as the sheer volume of U.S.–Japan relations expanded and much wider strata of the two countries came to be involved in them, the relative role of the service-school graduates naturally diminished. Nevertheless, they continue to remain important in all areas of interaction between the two countries.

This is particularly the case with those who went into professions that involve relations with Japan. The largest single group of this kind is those whose careers have been in the governmental service, particularly in the diplomatic. Quite a few have reached high positions there in connection with Japan, several as high as deputy chief of mission, or consul-general in Okinawa, or chief of the Japan desk in the State Department. Three even went on to ambassadorial posts, although these were outside Japan. Only one, so far as I know, has served in the legislative branch—Congressman Samuel Stratton of upstate New York, who went through the navy language school. Among those who went into business, many have had careers that involved them with Japan in varying degrees.

In 1971, the *Asahi Shimbun*, Japan's leading daily, did a series of articles on the United States and Japan, which eventually was published as a book. Early in this series, the *Asahi* tries to get at the difference between the several generations of Americans involved intimately with Japan. I do not remember exactly what I said during one of the many interviews we went through, but this is how they quote me (whom they describe as a representative of the "second generation"): "We are unavoidably influenced, to a greater or lesser degree, by our memories of the war. Our sense of closeness to the Japanese as former adversaries, and our sense of responsibility to them during the Occupation, combined with feelings of caution remaining in the backs of our minds, operate at times to make us appear officious or to be saying one thing to Americans and another to the Japanese. The attitudes of the third-generation Japanologists, in contrast, are more distant and abstract." The *Asahi* then goes on to say: "The third generation is aware of no lingering shadows of the Pacific War," . . . it shares "none of the patronizing 'let us teach you and guide you' attitude of its predecessors . . . " but "approaches Japan directly, coolly, and objectively, as an object of study."

As is the case with most generalizations, there is undoubtedly some truth in these, but on the whole they are somewhat overdrawn. It is true that we came out of the war with a strong sense of adversary relationship. Nevertheless, as I have already noted in some of the typical experiences of newly arrived American soldiers in Japan fresh from the combat areas, the hostile attitudes very quickly gave way to something quite different. In part this was because of the unhostile and even friendly behavior of the Japanese people, their cooperative manner, and, what cannot be disregarded, the deliberate blandishing and seduction of Americans. Combat veterans, filled with fearful hostility, soon found themselves without targets and quickly became friendly, some of them even becoming advocates of Japan when they finally returned home.

It is a curious characteristic of Americans that they often

become advocates of the countries they are involved with. Perhaps that very involvement is the sign of a preexisting natural affinity. Before World War II, for example, there was a sharp division in the State Department between the "China hands" and the "Japan hands," each group acting as advocate of "its" country. The China hands were very hostile toward Japan, favored strong, almost punitive, postwar measures, and were inclined to radical solutions such as the abolition of the emperor system; the Japan hands, on the contrary, favored dealing with the "better" elements of Japanese society, more conciliation, more attention to the structural realities of Japanese life, and the retention of the emperor system. And so it was that many of the Americans who served in the Occupation became the advocates of the country they were there to rule. American Occupationnaires were often accused back home of being too friendly to the Japanese, of having been taken into camp, of having been seduced by their charges.

There may be something to this, particularly among those who held positions of responsibility. It should be remembered that many Americans found themselves suddenly catapulted into positions that gave them enormous powers, sometimes greater than those of the very highest-ranking officials of the government of Japan. Some of these positions were at a cabinet, or at least a subcabinet, level. Most of the Americans who held these positions had, on the face of it, little background that would qualify them for such high posts. But what is remarkable is that they nevertheless managed to perform with extraordinary competence. A man like Wolf Ladejinsky, for example, who, until the end of the war had held a modest position in the Foreign Agriculture Division of the United States Department of Agriculture, was, if not the father, then the godfather of land reform in Japan. In that position, he had the powers of a minister of agriculture, of the supreme advisor to the chief of state (then, in effect, General MacArthur). Or Theodore Cohen, early on the chief of the Labor Division of the Economic and Scientific Section, whose only formal qualification for this position was that he had written his master's thesis at Columbia University on the history of the Japanese labor movement. He had the responsibility for guiding the basic postwar reforms in the field of labor through the ample minefields of the right and the left, which included the *Yomiuri* Newspaper strike, the threatened national railway strike, and the general strike set for February 1947. For a young man in his late twenties, this was no mean achievement.

It was not, therefore, surprising that many of the top Occupationnaires felt a strong sense of responsibility and a certain protectiveness about Japan, particularly against the many pressures constantly coming from the United States. Some of them were also, no doubt, all too ready to offer gratuitous and pompous advice to the Japanese; but it should not be forgotten that they were very often called upon for this advice, whether sincerely or manipulatively, and such habits do not die easily. Perhaps more than any of these things, those of us who held responsible positions in the Occupation—even if they were somewhat less than of cabinet level—found ourselves extremely attentive to everything that was happening in the country. I used to have the feeling that I could not rest in the morning until I read all the news available, or heard it on the radio, or picked up the information reports that were constantly circulating around our offices. We had a sense that we were involved in, or connected with, everything that was going on in Japan. I wanted to know what was happening in remote areas; it seemed terribly urgent for me to understand the fluctuations of the economic situation in Niigata Prefecture; school registration rates in Kyoto senior high schools seemed to me of the utmost importance; and I simply had to know about the state of the early spring herring runs off the coast of Rumoi and Mashike in Hokkaido. After all of that, the return to the United States was a great letdown. I can still remember the sudden feeling of disengagement I had on my first trip back to America when I woke up one morning to find that I had lost that sense of vital relation to the news.

These are parts of the experience of my generation, both of

language officers or scholars and of people who served in the Occupation. *Asahi*'s "third generation" may have missed something by not knowing about the war and the Occupation, except in history books.

Whatever the case may be, they take for granted many of the things that for us were problematical or that still seem strange. When I see well-scrubbed and well-dressed young Japanese boys and girls in their expensive and stylish clothes, another image sometimes comes to mind: of the shabby, misshapen, pick-me-up clothes their parents and grandparents wore right after the war. Sometime late in 1947 or early 1948, when there had been a slight relaxation in the desperateness of postwar scarcity, I was out for a stroll with a famous Tokyo University professor. Just as we crossed the street in midtown Tokyo, Professor K. turned toward me and asked to feel the fabric of the civilian jacket I was wearing. "Such fine material," he said dreamily, as he fingered the jacket. "How much did it cost you?" "Thirty dollars," I said, which was at that time just over ten thousand yen, a princely monthly salary. "Do you think you could buy one for me?" he asked. As it happened, I could not, but I was impressed by his willingness to spend a whole month's salary on a jacket. This was my first intimation that the "postwar" was beginning to thaw out. The younger generation of Americans —and of Japanese, too—takes these things for granted. It assumes that it is natural for Japanese to be well—and expensively—dressed. I do not.

Many other things give me double vision—seeing a petulant young lady pushing aside a half-eaten bowl of rice, for example, and then remembering how important it used to be to eat every last grain of rice in your bowl. Or seeing grossly fat Japanese people on the streets or on television, or reading about diet schools, diet courses, or weight-reducing schools. These seem perfectly natural to young people today. But not to me.

Another double vision: these days, when Americans are so entranced with Japanese management methods and quality control, I remember that in the late 1940s, quality control and

190

quality control circles were considered to be American managerial concepts. The American statistician Dr. W. Edwards Deming, who visited Japan as a consultant to the American Occupation, preached about it constantly. The Japanese took these ideas seriously and then adapted them to their needs. In recognition of Dr. Deming's contribution to the development of quality control ideas, a Japanese Deming Prize was established in 1950 by major companies and awarded every year for important achievement in this field. Today, we Americans think of these as Japanese ideas, and American firms and management experts are trying to adapt them to the American manufacturing process.

The younger generation of American scholars takes for granted the bustling, garish, restless, chrome-plated synthetic scene that constitutes so much of modern Japan. I do not. I still remember the constraint, the tranquillity, and the austere, *shibui* quality of life, even in war-destroyed Japan, and I wonder where it has gone. In front of me now, as I sit writing this in Tokyo, I see a small enclave of older houses clinging precariously to little pieces of green surrounded by menacing masses of concrete, glass, and steel blazing in peeling colors of Mediterranean white and blue, metallic copper, green mustard, reddish brown, and pale lavender—all faintly streaked by smog. Even these survivors are all painted, and in some cases the roof tiles are blue or they have corrugated tin roofs.

One of the great revelations of my life when I first came to Japan was to discover how beautiful unpainted wood could be. Today, when I visit a country village, I find all the houses painted; unpainted wood remains here and there only as a sign that a family is too poor to afford paint, not as a sign of a deliberately chosen aesthetic preference. In one of my favorite fishing villages in Chiba Prefecture, all of the roofs used to be a uniform earthy tile color. From afar, this gave the village an aesthetic unity that was very striking. Today, all this is changed. Some fifteen years ago or more some enterprising salesman succeeded in convincing the local residents that their roofs should be "colorful" (how alien the term is to traditional Japanese aesthetic concepts may be seen in the fact that it is expressed in English, pronounced *karafuru*), not the traditional drab earth color. So just as soon as a family did well economically, it would replace the old ceramic tiles with garish electric-blue roofing. To the family newly experiencing this prosperity, the colorful roof is a sign of modernity, a signal to neighbors and to the world that it has arrived. But to me it is only another sign of the disappearance of an older Japanese aesthetic that had always been one of Japan's greatest contributions to the world. It is as if the older aesthetic of restraint and *shibui* were only a phenomenon of scarcity and poverty, not a deliberately chosen canon of taste. When the Japanese were poor, the traditional tastes prevailed. When they become rich, the national taste becomes *nouveau-riche.*

These examples suggest some of the ambivalence in my generation's view of modern, successful Japan. We have had a strong effect on American studies of Japan, and therewith on world scholarship. We have even had some effect on Japanese scholarship itself, on how Japanese scholars look at their own society. We have played a role, important even if modest, in the relations between the United States and Japan. To these we have brought our own mixture of light and dark, substance and shadow. Our successors do not have the same mix of experiences; they bring their own to the relation.

In the end, our language school experience may or may not have been important to society and the world. The judgment is partly a subjective one, and partly still awaits the further outcome of events. But it was certainly important to those of us who went through it and probably to many of those we may have affected by our actions. We ourselves came out of the experience very different from what we were when we went into it.

I, for example, learned patience. I learned how to relax, how to interact without words, how to pace myself, how to achieve composure and tranquillity under pressure. You will not believe that I could learn these things from the Japanese, given their current reputation for being such a restless people, hard driven (as in the Datsun Motor television commercial: "We are driven!"), so often unable to relax. But in the past, many Japanese had mastered these skills, much more than today— whether from the disciplines of religious contemplation, intense training, or a less modern image of the relation of the self and its needs to society—and I was lucky to learn from them. Beneath the surface of restlessness, many Japanese still know how to achieve relaxation. Those who do not, have experienced an irreparable loss, comparable to the loss of the traditional aesthetic.

I also discovered the virtues of decent restraint. The heart does not have to be worn on the sleeve, the innermost secrets need not be blared forth to the world to prove that we have strong feelings or to show our sincerity. I also learned that one need not impose one's private worries, problems, and pains on unwilling others. In other words, I discovered another aspect of the traditional Japanese concept of *omoiyari*, "awareness of and consideration for others."

I hope others have benefited from my—or our—experiences. I hope our respective countries have benefited—and I believe that, if only in a modest way, they have. But even if they have not, it should, I think, be clear that I have.

定価3,200円

in Japan